Thinking Fishing

Chris Sheldon

Dave + Nikki,
Best wishes!

Always wondering 'why'?

Not, 'Why we go fishing'; everyone writes about that…
but 'why do we catch? Why does it work? What can I
do when it doesn't?'

Thinking Fishing

Some of the articles in 'Thinking Fishing' were first published in *Countrymans Weekly*, and have been reviewed and edited prior to inclusion to ensure they remain up to date. The 'Resurgent River Tame' article originally appeared in '*Staffordshire Life*'.

ISBN: 9781720252412

Cover design by Joe Watson at JW Illustration
www.joewatsonillustration.com

Book and print formatting by Jo Harrison
www.ebook-formatting.co.uk

Acknowledgements

My thanks go to Steve Lowrie and the team at Countrymans Weekly, and to Louise Elliot, then editor at Staffordshire Life, for actually printing some of my ramblings. Also to 'Her Ladyship' for tolerating all this – thanks Jayne – and to my girls, Laura and Jess. Thanks also to Joe Watson at JW Illustration for the cover, and to my book formatter, Jo Harrison.

Some of the anglers I've been privileged to share a bank with over the years; Andy Plackett, Ben Harker, Mark Wilton, Loz Watton, Mark Robins, Chris Timothy, my brother Martin; Ken Goldingay, Bob Sanders, the fly tying phenomenon that was the late Peter Knight. Thank you, gentlemen.

Finally, to Dad, for actually taking me fishing 44 years ago. And to Mum, who spent the next 12 years going on holiday to where the fishing was good, rather than the weather…

"Angling may be said to be so like Mathematics, that it can never be fully learnt"

Izaak Walton, The Compleat Angler, 1653

For Laura

Preface

As 2010 drew to a close, the UK experienced its coldest ever December. I was managing a fishery at the time, and coaching fly fishing, and some coarse fishing as well. For weeks the temperature stayed well below zero, and it never seemed to get properly light. Everything was frozen solid; for a bet, a local chap rode a bike along the frozen canal between Fazeley and Huddlesford. I'd written an article on fly fishing for a website as a favour; it was well received, and as I sat bemoaning the freezing weather, I sketched out a few more. A phone call to the then Editor of the *Countrymans' Weekly* newspaper resulted in a few being published, and I started to wonder if I could actually do this properly…

It's now 2017 and I'm still wondering. Some of the articles in 'Thinking Fishing' have been published before in the *Countrymans Weekly*. The article on the 'Resurgent River Tame' originally appeared in *'Staffordshire Life'*. The rest of the book is new material.

I caught my first fish aged 4. In the subsequent 40 plus years I've fished for both coarse and game fish all over the UK and Ireland; in Africa, Goa and (briefly) the Caribbean. Having enjoyed match fishing in my teens and early 20's, I turned to fly fishing for a change, qualifying as an instructor in 2006. I've taught ever since, both coarse and game, mainly young people and those with learning difficulties.

This wonderful, diverse sport of ours continues to surprise. You never stop learning. And I've always wondered – Why? Why didn't I catch today? Why did the bites dry up? Why did that Trout turn away at the last minute? Why did my float move like that? Why did changing my hook / leader / depth / bait make such a difference…?

I hope this book answers a few of those sorts of questions. If you aren't an angler, or are a beginner, I hope it makes you think, perhaps even inspires you a little. If you love this sport as much as I do, I do hope this book gives you something to think about.

Contact Me:

If you could post a review on Amazon, I'd be grateful. It's always good to hear from people, whatever they have to say. Despite my ongoing dislike of social media and the issues that accompany it's use (or misuse!), I do have a website, and occasionally post something on Twitter. The website has an email link, please feel free to contact me if you have a comment or question.

And thank you - for reading my book.

www.thinkingfishing.co.uk

Contents

Arranging every article I've ever written, plus a few others, into some sort of order has been difficult. After much deliberation, I've split the book into three sections. Please - don't avoid the Trout section if you're a Coarse angler, and vice versa; I wanted this to be about getting anglers to *think* about their fishing, which might mean you end up reading, and subsequently trying, something new and different...

Coarse Fishing

Weirs

There is something magical about a weir, or more specifically, the Weirpool. They're compelling. They have to be fished.

Weirs used to be an essential part of river management. Simple, shallow ones can be used to hold back the rivers flow, creating a slower, deeper area above. Below the weir, the cascade creates a deep, well oxygenated pool, the effects of which are noticeable for quite a way downstream. Temporary weirs can be used to remove silt and debris, as the weirpool scours the river bed clean. Moving the weir downstream in stages can clean whole sections of river of years of accumulated silt and rubbish, exposing clean gravel underneath.

Years ago, weirs were created to drive mill wheels. Called 'races', these narrowed, fast sections of river drove the water wheel more efficiently. Often these mill races created scoured, clean pools below. The classic 'Mill Pond' or pool, was usually found above the weir, where water was held up, building a 'head' of water to cascade over the weir and drive the wheel. Mill Ponds were often stocked, especially in the Middle Ages, with Carp, for food.

Weirs were also used to create pools for fishing, especially for Trout, and an excellent example of this is on the Dove at Milldale, in the Peak District. As the river tumbles down through the dale, losing height quite rapidly, a weir every 25 yards or so creates a series of pools, the pool below a weir also forming the head of the next weir along. It's a bit like a series of steps. Each pool holds a resident stock of fish. This stretch at Milldale is hallowed ground, described in detail in Izaak Walton's 'The Compleat Angler'. Some of the weirs date back many hundreds of years.

Old, almost derelict mill pools and weirs have held a fascination for anglers for years. The inhabitants of these pools achieve a mythical status locally. Stories of child - eating Pike and serpent like Eels are commonplace. As I wrote earlier – they simply *have* to be fished.

There is an old millpool and weir on the River Sow, at Great Bridgeford. Our club has the lease, and despite the inevitable tales of monster Chub etc, hardly anyone ever fishes it. I went to have a look.

It was easy to see why few anglers made the effort. The millpool above the weir is overgrown with willows and alder; very little of it was visible, let alone fishable. The weir itself was at right angles to the pool and created a drop of several feet; the boiling, seething cauldron below was a mass of bubbles and foam. The pool created (correctly called the 'Tail Race') had flows heading in different directions and was complete chaos. 20 yards further on everything came together, slowed down, and the river continued on its way, clear and weedy. The bank I had access to was separated from the main flow and the weir by a strip of water maybe 6 inches deep, and 20 feet across. Wading was out of the question; that 6 inches of water covered easily 3 feet of silt.

These days, I like fishing places like this. I enjoy the challenge; presenting a bait, even getting a bait into the water, is difficult enough, let alone actually catching anything.

Originally, I tried running a float through. I managed to clamber through the undergrowth to kneel on the concrete at the edge of the weir itself. Despite the overhanging trees I could drop a float into the bubbles at the base of the weir and hopefully let the current take the float downstream. Bulked shot a foot above the hook was intended to get the bait down quickly. I caught a few small Perch, but struggled to control the float, and I had no idea where my loosefeed was going. And the noise from the weir was deafening. After ½ hour I'd had enough, and moved to the quieter end of the pool.

As I described, wading was out of the question. I elected to throw a swimfeeder upstream, into the area below the weir, a difficult cast with overhanging trees. I had to put the rod on a rest, pointing up into the sky, to keep the line clear of the shallows and in direct contact with the 'feeder. A few small Perch inevitably followed and then a change from maggots to Luncheon Meat on the hook resulted in a savage take, pulling the rod off its rest. I missed it. I still don't know how.

A few casts later on the quiver tip pulled round and I hit it as it was still moving. Something heavy moved downstream towards me, putting a proper bend in the rod. It turned and ran back up to the weir, causing the clutch on my ageing Mitchell 300 to slip. Then it gave a huge, vicious tug and the line snapped. 6lb breaking strain Maxima, not just stretched and broken, but properly smashed.

I sat back to think, lost in that moment of despair that follows losing something big. Chub? Barbel? Not fast enough. A big Bream would explain the heaviness, the weight, but even a really big one doesn't put up much of a fight. Big Trout maybe? Currently, I'm thinking Carp – and it wouldn't have to be a huge one. No-one has ever caught a Carp in the Sow as far as the club is aware. Is this how these legends begin, I wondered?

Well, there's something big and heavy below the weir in the River Sow at Great Bridgeford. It snaps 6lb Maxima with ease, has probably still got a number 10 Kamasan hook in it, and if anyone manages to catch it, I'd like to know what it is!

Inspiration – from the pen of the great Richard Walker

The late, great Richard Walker would occasionally publish his articles (mainly from the *Angling Times*) in a book, as a compilation. I inherited one of these, titled 'Walkers Pitch' as a nine year old. I say 'inherited'; what I really mean is I borrowed it from my Dad and never returned it.

I would urge any angler to get hold of a copy. Published in 1959 or thereabouts, it is, without doubt, one of the best angling books I've ever read. For those, possibly younger, readers that don't know of Richard Walker, he was best known as holder of the British Carp record (a 44lb fish from Redmire Pool), and as a writer. He also invented the first electric bite alarm, and the ubiquitous 'Arlesey Bomb' leger weight. He was known as one of the first anglers to apply logical, scientific thought to his fishing.

In 'Walkers Pitch' there is an article, titled simply '*small river fishing*' which could have been written about, or rather for, my local river Mease. As a boy, I'd often read this before setting off for the river. It didn't take much imagination to link the river RW described to the Mease. The swims he wrote about (I think he was referring to rivers like the Upper Ouse or possibly the Ivel, where he spent a lot of his time) also existed in the Staffordshire countryside, and I'm sure they do in the upper reaches of any lowland river. RW writes about a small river, full of chub, roach, perch and pike, plus 'the occasional trout'. Trout, for me, back in the late seventies / early eighties, were something wealthy people fished for on the river Test. They were certainly not on my list of target species back then! Yet, here was the great Richard Walker, telling me that rivers like the Mease held trout, and I could go and catch them. Suitably inspired, I spent weeks fishing worms, catching lots of Perch but failing dismally to catch a Brownie. (I did eventually catch a trout from the Mease, many years later, from the old mill pool at Clifton. I was after chub at the time. As far as I know, no-one has seen or caught one since!).

This book, Walkers Pitch, became something of a bible for me. There is another chapter, all about Pike; RW recalls a fishing trip with his Grandfather, who used to catch Pike, oddly, when he was fishing for Roach. His logic, simply, was that the Pike would be where the Roach were. In other words, where their food was. Many years ago, aged about 13, I was fishing another of my local rivers, the Anker, catching roach. It was easy; run a stickfloat down the middle, single maggot on an 18, feed every other cast. I remember two pike anglers turning up, fishing sprat deadbaits. They were struggling, in a river that's known to be full of Pike. Eventually, about to pack up, I summoned the courage to speak to these two 'grown ups'… 'try here' I suggested.' It's full of roach'. Their response was, well, patronising at best. But as I left, one of them did throw his deadbait out where I'd been fishing. He had a run immediately, and netted a decent Pike a few minutes later. (I did try not to look smug, I really did…)

I still read Walkers Pitch today. Another article, about using bread as a bait, really got me thinking. RW explains about using what he calls 'balanced crust'. In the article, he talks about how bread crust will float (classic Carp method, floating crust ; works for Chub too!), but bread 'flake', the white bit, will sink. He worked out, back in the 50's, that if you got a bit of bread flake with the crust still attached, you could arrange it to 'pop-up' off the bottom. Today's Carp anglers spend a fortune trying to achieve this, using 'neutral density' boilies and 'popups'.

I often use balanced crust, on the Mease, for Chub. Find a swim about 2 feet deep, running fairly quickly, and clear. There should be just enough depth so the surface doesn't ripple, and you can see the bottom. I try to position my balanced crust on the bottom in between the beds of 'streamer weed', where I can see it. The Chub patrol along this stretch, en route from one deep hole to another. Stop a small bomb or other leger weight about six inches from the hook, make sure your cast is slightly downstream, and the balanced crust will pop up, angled because of the current, about 4 inches off the bottom. The Chub practically swim into it. You don't need an indicator of any sort – you can see the fish take the bait and turn downstream with it. It's exciting stuff.

Writing this, and re-reading Walkers Pitch again, especially the balanced crust article, has really got me thinking. The book was published in the fifties, and I can still find it relevant and inspirational today. Is there anything new in angling? If you can, get hold of a copy of Walkers Pitch. An good, original copy from 1959 is worth upwards of £60, but it was reprinted in a limited edition in 2003 by The Little Egret Press; these copies are more affordable. Wonder if Dad would like his original back?

The Centre Pin

Nearly every coarse angler uses a fixed spool reel, and I'm no exception. My personal favourite is the venerable Mitchell 300 type, which was made from the 1950's up until about 1990 in its original form. An unbelievable 30 million Mitchell 300's and derivatives were produced, and at one point the factory was making an incredible 12,000 reels a day. The company founder was a clock maker by profession, and the quality of the gearing and the components was superb. I could talk, or write, for hours about the 300, the 440 Match, the 810, the 300S and so on. My favourite 300 is nearly as old as me.

I've used Mitchell reels all my angling life. As a fly fisherman I've always used reels designed specifically for that, and when I've dabbled in sea fishing I've tried Multipliers. For stick float fishing on rivers I think the original ABU501 closed-face reel is perfect, and I still use an old 501 today. But one reel type I'd never owned and never learned to use, is the Centre Pin.

The centre pin is so called because of its construction. It is a very simple, very basic design. A drum, or 'spool', fits over a spindle (the 'pin'), about which it can spin, hindered only by the anglers finger or thumb. A bit like one of those 1970's executive toys, once you set it spinning it keeps going, almost like perpetual motion.

Modern 'pins actually run on a needle roller bearing, as do most fly reels which are of a similar construction. The true centre pin, however, is simply a spool fitted over a spindle – no bearing. Just a thin film of grease or oil is all there is between the two. (The fly reel is different in other ways - they often incorporate a drag mechanism as well as a simple 'check' or ratchet, and a bearing to support the extra weight and load that a simple pin would struggle to bear.)

Running a simple stick float, or a heavier Avon type, along the inside track of a fast, pushy sort of river like the upper Trent or Severn, is a perfect scenario for the 'pin. The current is fast enough to pull the line directly off the spool, with no assistance or involvement from the angler. If you've never done this, you can't appreciate it. It's a pure, almost magical experience, and today, that's what Centre pin reels are known for - trotting floats on rivers.

Playing a fish on a centre pin is another matter entirely. There is no gearing or drag; one turn of the spool equals one turn's worth of line retrieved, or given. Contrast that to a fixed spool reel where one handle turn is geared to 5 or more revolutions of the bale arm! With a 'pin there is no mechanical intervention, which contributes to the 'pure' experience I mentioned earlier.

Obviously, back in the days before the fixed spool, everyone used a 'pin, because that was all there was. So that's stillwaters as well as rivers. And that got me thinking....

I wondered if this association between the centre pin and running water was justified. Is it just that because the 'pin is so perfect, so suited, for river work that we've forgotten it can be used on stillwaters too? I do a lot of my coarse fishing on small pools, chasing Tench, Crucian carp, and their larger cousins. Why not use a centre pin for that?

So I went and bought one. It's a cheap, mass produced item, cost about £30 in a sale, nothing like the hand built works of art that go for thousands. I was childishly happy with it, and couldn't wait to try it out.

The first thing I discovered is that casting, as we know it, is a complete non-starter. There is a technique called the 'Wallis Cast', and another called the 'Nottingham Cast'. The Wallis Cast especially is an art form that is beyond me. The idea is that you cast in the normal way, but 'bat' the reel with your hand to start it spinning and release line. In theory, the tackle flies through the air at a speed that matches the rate at which the reel releases it. Done properly, it is wonderful to watch. All it does for me is create tangles and 'birds nests' like I'd never seen before.

A conversation with my Dad, now in his seventies and with a lifetime of fishing behind him, revealed another technique. You pull line off the reel and coil it neatly into a pile on the ground next to you. You trap the line against the rod with your finger, and then cast, allowing the coil of line to unravel and run through the fingers of your left hand as it does so. I tried it, and it works, although a Centre Pin Purist wouldn't appreciate it.

Luckily for me, fishing close in on a lake for Tench or running a float down the inside on a river doesn't require casting as such, you just swing the float out into place. My first attempt with my new toy, on the Tame, taught me one lesson straight away. You can forget using your lightweight 3 no. 4 shot stick floats or traditional quills or whatever - you need something heavy. I ended up using an Avon pattern taking about 4 AAA, which helped pull the line off the reel along with the current. It worked well; by controlling the speed of the drum with my thumb, I could slow the float down so it was moving fractionally slower than the current. I used to try to do this with a closed face reel, with limited success, but with the 'Pin it was easy. (Slowing the float down allows the hookbait to catch the float up - normally the float precedes the bait by some margin, especially in fast water).

Next trip was to a favourite Carp pool - sunny day, warm, perfect conditions for freelined floating crust. A few dog biscuits scattered in the margins were soon being taken, and I dropped a bit of crust a few feet in front of the nearest Carp. He obligingly sucked it in, making that trademark slurping noise, and then the Avon rod hooped over as he ran for the lily bed twenty yards away. Now another valuable lesson! You must have the 'check' engaged or the ultimate in tangles, and a lost fish, is inevitable. The check is a primitive ratchet and pawl mechanism that slows the drum down, making a sort of clicking noise as it does so. If it's engaged, the drum won't run away with you. in other words, the spool won't 'overrun'.

As I mentioned earlier, actually playing a decent fish on a 'Pin is a very different experience. Somehow, you feel more; it's more 'connected'. I've used it often this summer and have plans to do more river work this autumn. It will never replace my beloved Mitchell 300, or the ABU501, but I'm really glad I bought one. You should, too.

Lighten the Load

A few years ago, I was given the opportunity to fish a private bit of the river Trent that had, allegedly, not seen an angler on its banks in living memory. Some bits of the Trent, and the Tame, Dove and other Staffordshire rivers, are buried deep in inaccessible farmland and have always been unfished. Clubs never tendered for the fishing rights, as actually getting to the bank usually required a tractor or a Land Rover. Obviously I jumped at the chance to fish, and arranged a date in early July that should have seen the river in its summer prime.

The night before I even abstained from my usual bottle of red…. this was a special opportunity; rarely do anglers get the chance to fish a 'virgin' stretch of water. The car was loaded the night before, bait acquired, alarm clocks set….

I should point out that for the preceding 12, 15 years or so my coarse angling exploits had been restricted to the occasional match and the odd evening session when camping with my daughter. I had become almost exclusively a trout fisherman, and was seriously out of practice.

My coarse kit was in good order, if a little dated, and I loaded the car confident that whatever the river threw at me I could deal with. A stick float run down the inside was my preferred tactic, loosefeeding maggots. If I needed to fish a feeder in the middle I could do that; waggler on the far bank would be ok, even a bomb fished tight into the margins if the need arose. Bait was red and bronze maggots, sitting in their separate containers on the cool concrete of the garage floor. (The days of leaving maggots in the fridge overnight are long gone; Her Ladyship, supported by The Aged Parent and numerous other female family members, has issued an edict…)

The following morning, I was up, out and on my way in record time. The weather was perfect. Overcast, and a gentle breeze. It was going to be a good day…

You're probably thinking this is going to be one of those once in a lifetime tales of a huge netful of 1lb plus Roach, big Chub, Barbel, and the occasional bonus Brown Trout etc. Well, it isn't. There is a 'but' coming, and it's a big one….

It is true that I was thinking that this would be a once in a lifetime opportunity. The people that owned the stretch had sold it to a gravel company and I knew that any access to it in future would be non-existent. The Trent here is weedy, and fast, and if you can find a 'run' between the weeds, perfect for Chub.

I parked up, unloaded the car… and then the problems began. I sat by the side of the lane, ready to heave my kit over the gate, and realised that I was going to have to walk along the edge of three fields, across several irrigation ditches, and over several fences. My kit, designed for moving short distances over the well laid paths of a commercial fishery or canal towpath, was immovable.

I had a rod holdall, a seat box system, a bait coolbag, a net holdall, and the seat box mounted on a trolley arrangement you pulled behind you. Perfect for a match, or a day, at Baden Hall or Heronbrook, or on one of those venues where you can almost drive to your peg.

Definitely not what you need for several miles of inaccessible farmland!

Giving up was not an option. Obviously, the seat box and trolley would have to go. I started to reload the car. As I methodically ditched tackle, rapidly filling up the car, I realised that this wasn't about what I could do without. It was more about what I actually *needed*.

I eventually arrived on the bank wearing, rather than carrying, my waders, and clutching a made up rod and a landing net. My pockets were stuffed with bits and pieces, spare hooks, disgorger and so on, and my bait was in a carrier bag along with a bottle of water and some sandwiches. The walk, easily a mile over the margins of fields, over ditches, hedges and so on, was exhausting, and I knew there was no way I could have done it with all my kit.

Determined to fish, I set up, threw in some maggots and ran the float through on a line just past the rod tip. It was great; really enjoyable, simple and straightforward. I caught a few, mainly Roach and some Chub, and lost loads of tackle in the weeds and overhanging branches. I really enjoyed myself. I realised that a lot of the things I would think about normally, didn't apply. For example, I couldn't have the 'shall I try a feeder for a Barbel' conversation with myself because I didn't have the right tackle with me. I couldn't ponder whether to try a different bait, or different rig, because everything else was in the car. I could focus on the job in hand, and also notice what was going on around me. It was more enjoyable; almost liberating - less like work, more like the pleasure it's supposed to be.

Returning home, tired but inspired, I put together a set of kit that I could easily carry. One bag, one rod, and a landing net. My next few trips were a real pleasure, and as the months wore on, I found myself carrying less and less. I started doing a lot more coarse fishing, simply by making it easier and more accessible. I added a decent chair to the kit list, and restricted my reel selection to a single Mitchell 300 with three spools, loaded with 5, 8 and 12lb breaking strain lines. The rod was a John Wilson Rovex Avon 'travel rod', with seperate quiver tip and Avon top sections. At 11', I could even use it as a spinning rod if I fancied trying for Pike or Perch. Plus the fact it would do for ledgering, float fishing or freelining. I knew I'd miss the length if I was fishing a stick float but to be honest, I managed. I filled a small tackle box with floats, shot and hooks to nylon, plus a few more odds and ends. After a while I realised my heaviest item of kit was my big flask of tea, but there was no way I was leaving that behind...

This new kit lives in the car permanently. I can be fishing within a few minutes of parking up, as long as I don't have to walk far. I've started to enjoy impromptu sessions with no planning beforehand, especially of a summers evening when I can stalk Carp or Chub with freelined baits. Occasionally I've stopped at a pool or bit of river with no bait at all, and used whatever I could scavenge from the hedges and grassland around the margins. I used to revel in being able to move about when flyfishing, working my way around a lake; I'm doing that now when I'm coarse fishing, and its great fun. Try it!

Chub – 'the fearfullest of fishes….'

I've written before about 'Walkers Pitch', the classic collection of the great Richard Walker's 'Angling Times' columns from the 1950's. It's essential reading, I think, for any angler. There is a chapter entitled 'Roach and Chub', which always puzzled me, as the two species are so different.

One anecdote from the chapter concerns Chub, and it's one I've always remembered. RW describes being directed to a swim where an enormous Chub had been seen earlier. The fish was there, but "it saw me" he wrote, "and vanished. I settled down to wait for him to come back. They nearly always do… Chub come 'unscared', at about 10 minutes to the pound!"

Izaak Walton describes the Chub as the 'fearfullest of fishes' and writes about how even the shadow of a bird passing overhead can send a shoal of chub scattering like leaves in a gale.

All of the above leads me to a question. Why is this nervous, wary, easily frightened fish so easy to catch?

The answer is simple – the Chub is the greediest, least fussy, most voracious fish there is. It would be pointless compiling a list of 'best Chub baits' – they'll eat practically anything. You name it, you can catch a Chub on it.

Primarily a river fish, Chub will feed all year round. They will feed, gregariously, in the freezing cold, or on the hottest day. They can be caught on a static bait (ledgered) or a moving one (under a stick float, say; or freelined crust). They'll take a livebait (maggots, worms etc), or a particle like sweetcorn or maize. They love Luncheon Meat, or Spam. A whole article could be written about foraging for 'naturals' and fishing with frogs, slugs, caterpillers or even woodlice as bait. And I haven't even started on artificials like pellets or pastes, or spinners, plugs or dry flies…

I have an ambition to catch a big one, the same as I do for Perch and Roach. A big Chub to me is 5lb plus, that's over 2 and a bit kilos if you're 'European' or under 40. I've caught several around the 4lb mark, but never managed a '5'. I've lost several that were probably well over 5lb, including a memorable one from the Anker that an inexperienced passer-by, trying to be helpful, knocked off the hook with the rim of the landing net. If I tell you it would have been a tight fit in the net, and was possibly over 6lbs in weight, you can imagine why I was speechless (for once) and the gentleman returned to his walk rather quickly.

So how would I go about catching my 'big one'? There are two ways of approaching this; you can try and seek out your target fish by fishing big baits on a sort of roaming approach, wandering about and trying likely 'holes' and snaggy swims. The bigger chub do tend to be solitary, and maybe the best tactic is to go looking for them. The second option is simply to start catching smaller ones, and keep feeding… the idea is that bigger fish will simply move upstream in search of their meal. Match anglers will tell you that building a swim in a river is the same as on a Stillwater, as the match progresses the fish get bigger…

Chub fanatic and lure enthusiast Loz Watton would tell you that a Pike spinner or spoon fished 'up and across' in winter is the best tactic, and he's accounted for many 4lb plus fish over the years from the Tame and Mease.

He's also an advocate of the traditional freelined black slug, which legend has it chub find irresistible. Even Richard Walker says so. But I've never caught on a slug, I just end up getting covered in sticky, horrible slug 'goo' …

This autumn, before the rains start colouring everything up and all the weeds and cover get washed away, I'm going to try the second option, but with a simple, but very effective 'twist'…

Here is The Plan… there is peg I can fish on the Tame, near Elford. It's quite pacey, about 3 feet deep, hard gravel bottom, and I can run a fairly heavy stick float or a small Avon type through just past my rod tip, between beds of streamer weed. My eyesight is such that after 20 yards I can't see the float, so I have to either wind in or use 'The Force' to detect a bite. (A bite from a chub you have, as Yoda would say). About 30 yards downstream is a collection of overhanging trees, shrubs and a raft of accumulated detritus. Underneath that lot, I hope, is my 5 pounder…

The idea is to fish the 20 yards I can see, feeding maggots heavily, as far upstream as I can throw. (A catapult may be a good idea). I know that the resident shoal of 12oz fish will feed avidly, and by placing them in a keepnet as I catch them I'm hoping that their place in the shoal will be taken by other fish from downstream, as they move up following my trail of loosefeed. Hopefully, my 5 pounder will be encouraged to move from underneath all those branches...

After a few hours and several pints of maggots I would expect to have a good number of fish in the net up to 2lb or so, with the odd Roach or Perch thrown in. Now for the 'twist'...

I have to assume that the larger fish are now there. Remember how greedy Chub are? Sometimes the simplest ideas have remarkable results... all you do, is change your hookbait, for something different and much bigger... Put on a big chunk of breadflake, or a big bunch of maggots rather than a single one. Or a worm. The theory is that greed overcomes caution and the bigger fish push the smaller ones out of the way to get at it...

It works. It's a recognised tactic amongst river anglers who are trying to be more selective. Will it catch me a 5 lb plus Chub? Don't know yet!

Chub - the saga continues!

Last year, I wrote about Chub, 'the fearfullest of fishes' according to Izaak Walton, and how I planned to target a big one from the River Tame. I've never caught a really big one. My 'personal best' or 'PB' if you're a Carp angler, is a 4½ lb, tatty, battle scarred old fish from the Mease. The big, 5lb plus 'animals' in the Tame and Trent have always eluded me.

My plan was to spend a day running a float past a raft of overhanging branches and accumulated debris, feeding vast quantities of maggots, and catching an increasingly larger stamp of fish, until, as the day drew to a close, the 5lb'er would hit the net.

It didn't work.

I still maintain my plan was a good one. Chub are greedy. The idea that a shoal of small fish will gradually be replaced by larger ones is sound. Any river match angler will tell you that a good tactic is to simply try a bigger bait occasionally - the biggest fish in the shoal will bully the smaller ones out of the way to get at it. I used to pinch a piece of bread from my sandwiches occasionally and use that. A larger fish would usually result.

I had several good sessions on the river. I caught lots! , but nothing above a couple of pounds. Why?

The big fish are there, of that there is no doubt. The river is now as clean and as fertile as it's ever been. The weed growth and water clarity are exceptional. On a sunny day for example, you can look over the side of the bridge at, say, Elford or Hopwas, and see the bottom. It's about 3 feet deep. (Or a metre, if you are that way inclined). You can see the bigger fish moving about, in and out of the weeds. Not just Chub, but good Roach, and Pike as well. Pike are thriving in the Tame. They aren't huge, a 'double' is a good fish, and a 15lb fish was caught a few years ago from the weir in Tamworth, but they are plentiful, especially around the 5 or 6lb mark.

During the most recent failed attempt to catch a bigger Chub, Loz Watton dropped by, allegedly to see how I was getting on but really only to take the mickey. I have to take some stick on this occasion, because Loz has more big river Tame Chub to his credit than anyone else

I know, so he's entitled to ridicule my netful of 'tiddlers'. Speaking to Loz about his Chub methods got me thinking about why I can't catch a big one; and the success of Pike should have been a clue. Sometimes I need to stop and look around once in a while!

My new theory, is that in the Tame at least, *all the big Chub are predatory.*

We've always known that Chub eat live things. Richard Walker wrote often about using a whole, live Crayfish as bait. 'I doubt' he said 'that there is a better bait for really big Chub'. That was in 1954, or thereabouts. They'll eat anything; frogs, slugs, caterpillars, flies, berries... anything. Remember as well that the Pike in the Tame are flourishing, down to an abundance of small, prey fish. So are our bigger Chub munching those small fish as well rather than run around after my tiny maggots and casters?

I know for a fact that these small fish exist in huge numbers. The land along the river between Tamworth and Alrewas is flood plain, and every year those fields are flooded sometimes for weeks at a time. After the water has receded the fields are covered in huge flocks of mewling seagulls, feasting on the thousands of fry left stranded by the falling water levels.

Another point is that of the actual species of prey fish. An old saying amongst Pike fishermen is that the best bait for a Pike, is another Pike. There is, possibly, some substance behind this old adage; if a predator eats another of the same species, the fact that they are chemically identical may make them easier to digest, less energy being expended on turning the prey into usable sugars and proteins. I think Chub are the dominant species in the river, so it stands to reason that the majority of the fry I mentioned earlier will be Chub.

The clinching bit of evidence for my new ' all big Chub eat only small fish' theory comes from Loz. Every river Tame Chub over 4lb he's ever caught, he's caught on a spinner, when fishing for Pike.

Shot and Shotting

The legendary match angler Tom Pickering, many years ago, visited Tamworth to talk to local anglers. It was one of these 'An Evening with' type affairs, held at the Foseco factory social club near Drayton Manor, and, aged about 13, I was there in the crowd with a load of mates, listening to the man who, in 1989, would win the World Championship.

I remember it well. Not just because of the talk, but because I nearly got thrown out. Let me explain…

After his presentation, questions were invited 'from the floor'. After a while, an elderly gentleman got to his feet, extinguished his cigarette (it was the 80's, remember), put down his pint of Mild, and asked Tommy to talk about shotting. It was, he rightly said, vitally important. Could he explain all about it? 'The kids', he said, 'needed to learn'…

I was offended. I knew how shotting 'worked'. I knew, and my mates did, about 'equivalents'; about how 2BB equalled 1 AAA, and so on. We'd done our homework, and we were good at this stuff. We thought about what we did, and applied what we learnt, tried new ideas, developed techniques. And here was this 'grown up' being so patronising I couldn't help myself. 'Speak for yourself' I said, loudly. You could have heard a pin drop. Everyone looked at me. My mate Andy decided I was on my own from then on and tried to hide. Brother Martin simply slid under the table and stayed there. All eyes were on me when, in a much more nervous tone, I added 'We know about shotting. Perhaps the gentleman is the one who needs to learn?'.

The club erupted, as dozens of people laughed, and applauded. I remember blushing bright red as comments like 'well said', and 'good for you' rang out above the din. The management, threatening to 'throw the kids out', thought better of it and after a short discussion, decided to clean glasses at the bar instead. Tommy Pickering was laughing too, and he gave me a 'thumbs up ' ; I recall being quite proud of that.

When the evening ended and we made good our escape, I remember feeling upset. Just because I was a 'kid', didn't mean I was ignorant. Today, working in a modern secondary school and knowing young people like I do, I'm constantly surprised by them, and how much they know, and also by how much they keep to themselves. Modesty is rife.

So, what is shotting? How does it work? Where do these weird acronyms like AAA and BB come from?

Well, there has always been a need, since angling was invented, to add weight to a fishing line. Initially, this was just to sink the bait, but then people realised that it could aid casting, and allow you to fish further from the bank. Lead ball, or 'shot', has been around since the invention of gunpowder, when the first primitive cannons were designed. After the first world war, anglers drilled holes in spent lead bullets and, threading them onto the line, created a primitive 'rolling leger', a technique which is still used today for Chub and Barbel on weedy, pacy rivers. Float fishermen identified a need for smaller weights that could be attached to the line, helping a bait to sink quickly and also 'cocking' a float to improve bite detection. Cutting a split into a small lead ball worked brilliantly; you simply put the line in the split, and squeezed it shut, fixing it in place.

The breakthrough came shortly afterwards, when lead shot manufacturers, whose customers were mainly manufacturers of shotgun cartridges, started to get enquiries from fishing tackle companies. The 'split' was created by the angler with a penknife, until that process became automated, and by the 1950's the split shot, based on the same shot used in shotguns, was commonplace.

The shot sizes were the same as those used in shotgun ammunition, where the shooter selected a shot size appropriate to the quarry. For example, Pigeon required a much smaller shot size than, say, Geese, with Duck or Rabbit somewhere in between. A shotgun cartridge is selected on the size of the shot, the length of the cartridge, and the total weight of the shot. In angling terms though, the real genius was looking at shot in terms of their individual weight, rather than their actual *size*…

Shot was sized from number 1, down to 12 or 13, with the smaller number indicating a larger size. Some even larger sizes had letters; BB, AAA, and SSG. Anything smaller than a number 8 was colloquially known as 'dust shot'; in fact a number 13 is so small I can barely see it, never mind the split in it to fix it to the line.

What the elderly gentleman was referring to in his question, was the matter of equivalence. Suppose you had a float that 'cocked' perfectly with 3 BB shot. It's necessary to have some smaller shot 'down the line', to help the baited hook sink, so you have to be able to work out which shot you can use, to make up the 3 BB total. A look at shot weights, and their numbers, quickly showed that if you ignored the odd numbers, everything fell neatly into place, like this:

Size	Weight	Equivalent
SSG	1.6g	2 x AAA
AAA	0.8g	2 x BB
BB	0.4g	2 x No4
No4	0.2g	2 x No 6
No6	0.1g	1 x No8 + 1 x No10
No8	0.06g	1 x No10 + 1 x No12
No10	0.04g	2 x No12
No12	0.02g	

This little chart, and the thinking behind it, is really important, and we knew, even as kids, how useful it could be. My favourite 3BB waggler float, used on local stillwaters for fishing maybe 2 or 3 rod lengths out, took 2BB and a No.4 shot around the float to lock it into place, the a No6 below halfway, a No.8 a foot below that, and a No.10 a few inches from the hook. If Rudd were around, feeding on the top and I wanted the hook to sink more quickly, I moved the No.4 down to join the No.6. By the time I was about 14 this was second nature, and many a happy hour was spent working out intricate shotting patterns in the back of a Maths exercise book.

I like to think that this appreciation of the 'technical' side of things is where 'Thinking Fishing' really began. We really started to appreciate how shotting patterns affected the way a baited hook moved in the water, which in turn affected how many bites you got and ultimately how many fish you caught. I realised, having watched goldfish in a tank, that a baited hook could be sucked in, and spat out again, in less than a second, and that having slack line between the float and hook would mean that the fish merely straightened the line, and never moved the float at all. Correctly placed shot would remove the slack. if you start getting your hook back with your maggot hookbait sucked dry, move some shot around!

I copied the equivalents shown above out on to the lid of my tackle box, in marker pen. Eventually I learnt them off by heart, but it was possibly the most useful bit of information I had. Feel free to copy it out yourself …!

Tench – take advantage of no close season

When the old close season was enforced, we had to wait until June 16 before we could fish, and the traditional 'early season' quarry was always the Tench.

Stories abound about early morning, monster Tench, caught from picturesque lakes and pools as the mist burnt off and the sun rose, golden and warm. It's almost a cliché. The bait was usually worms, bread flake, or sweetcorn, and the technique was always the fabled 'Lift Method' made famous by Richard Walker, Fred J.Taylor and co. in the 1950's.

Now that the close season only applies to rivers and canals, we can fish for Tench in May – which, provided Spring has arrived and it's starting to warm up, is the perfect opportunity. Some fish may have already spawned, which means they'll now be feeding well. Those hen fish that haven't yet spawned will be heavy, and if you want to catch a big one, this is the time.

Unmistakable with their bottle green / dark olive colouring, Tench are hard fighting, strong fish that demand some respect. They are exclusively bottom feeders, hoovering up bloodworms and invertebrates from the silt and mud in the bottom of ponds, lakes and slow, deep rivers. Their colouring means they are perfectly camouflaged against a muddy bottom, and in amongst reeds and lilies. Unlike carp, which enjoy basking in warm sunlight, Tench dislike bright light and will move into deeper water when the sun is well up. This is one reason why early mornings are traditionally the best time for Tench; with the sun low in the sky, the fish will be closer in.

Catching your Tench, as with so many other species, is about doing some basic things well. Attention to details make a bigger difference to Tench than many other species. Chub, for example, will eat practically anything, and the depth that bait is presented at isn't so important. If a Chub wants to eat your hookbait, he'll move about to get at it. Tench, however, require your bait to be on the bottom. If it's suspended an inch above it, you'll not catch.

Obviously, the easy option is to leger. A simple swimfeeder rig, cast tight to an island or reedbed some distance away, works well, especially if your casting is accurate enough to build up a 'carpet' of free offerings. For me, though, float fishing, close in, next to a lily bed is the way forward. There is something evocative about a float, showing orange against the background of green. I use an 11' 'Avon' style rod for this sort of fishing. My 12 and 13' match rods aren't powerful enough to keep a decent fish out of the weedbeds, and I don't need the length. Equally, Carp rods, with heavy test curves, don't really work with float tactics; they are designed for something completely different. I use a traditional fixed spool reel (an old Mitchell 300 is my favourite) and 5lb line is strong enough. Simple waggler floats are ideal (traditionalists would use a porcupine quill) and a 12 or 14 barbless hook. I always use a short (say 6 inch) hooklength of lighter nylon or fluorocarbon; 4lb breaking strain is about right. At least if I do get broken, I'll get the float back, and the fish will lose a barbless hook easily enough.

First, though, we need to find our Tench, and that means a lily bed or similar to fish next to. In May, we have a problem, because there may not be any lilies yet! Maybe in the south of England there are a few lily leaves breaking the surface, but here in Staffordshire we may still be a few weeks away from that. The Tench will still be there, however. So are the lilies, they just haven't reached the surface yet. The bottom few feet of water is still a jungle of stems and roots, and that is where the fish will be. We need to fish alongside this 'jungle', and this is where some local knowledge, or remembering a walk around last summer, comes into play.

Having decided on an area to fish, my first job is usually to put some bait in. Ideally, I'd do this in advance, maybe the evening before, but this isn't always possible and some venues ban pre-baiting anyway. Plus, you run the risk of someone innocently setting up in 'your' prebaited swim, beating you to it. (this has happened to me, more than once. Moral of the story, drink less wine and get up earlier!). I always introduce sweetcorn, with a few pellets if I have any. Casters are good, and are less likely to attract smaller fish. Red maggots work too, Tench love them, but be prepared to bump into other species as well. Corn is more selective; you'll avoid Perch, definitely, and small roach and bream. (Hint: buy the sweetcorn with 'no added sugar' if you can – no sticky fingers!)

Having done that, and tackled up, it's time for the technical bit. Remember we have to put our hookbait on the bottom. Accuracy is so important, and this is how I do it…

1. Set your float shallow, locked into place on the line with some shot around it, enough to 'cock' the float so there's enough of the tip showing.
2. Attach a plummet to the hook, and lower the rig into the water where you've baited up. Remember we're only fishing close in – no need to cast as such.
3. Obviously, the float will sink. Push the float up a foot or so, and try again. You want to set it so it's just breaking the surface. The line between float and hook will be tight, and straight – no slack. Try to mark the exact spot in your mind.
4. Remove the plummet. Push the float up another 6 inches. Add a number 4 shot to the hooklength 4 inches above the hook. This is your 'anchor',

and because you're overdepth, it won't affect your float.

That's it. 1 or 2 grains of corn on the hook, position the float exactly where you plumbed the depth, put the rod in a rest, with the butt resting on your knee, sit back and await developments!

Accuracy – Being pedantic makes a difference

Earlier this year, I produced an article on Tench fishing, and described how to accurately plumb the depth. I made the point that with Tench being exclusively a bottom feeding fish your bait needed to be actually on the bottom if you were to catch.

I went on to say:

"1 or 2 grains of corn on the hook, position the float exactly where you plumbed the depth, put the rod in a rest, with the butt resting on your knee, sit back and await developments" …

Only recently, reading it back, did I realise that I'd actually touched on something very important, and I'd not gone into detail. Apologies for that, now it's time to put that right.

I said "position the float exactly where you plumbed the depth". That is vital; so important… for several reasons. Lake beds are rarely flat and level. Plumbing the depth in a particular spot is essential if you're going to put a bait on the bottom, but that same act restricts you to fishing that exact spot – an area a foot square is about right. Putting your float in an area that small every time requires skill, and practice, and discipline. The 'I'll just try over there for a bit 'approach doesn't work… you have to have the confidence, the faith even, to stick to your chosen spot.

It isn't just because of the depth, either. Ask a match angler what makes the most difference, and they'll tell you it's all about feeding. Using loosefeed, groundbait, 'free offerings', whatever you choose to call it, is essential if you're going to attract fish to the spot you're fishing, encourage them to feed, and keep them there so you can catch them.

Feeding is part of the anglers art. It's difficult to get right, and it's worth trying to figure out why we feed and whats happening when we do. Most anglers remember to 'chuck a bit in' every so often. That's not usually good enough. Feeding has to entice, it has to attract. Once there, fish have to stay, and that's the tricky bit. Feed too much, they'll eat their fill and move off. Feed too little, they'll move away to find more.

Also, feeding promotes competition amongst the fish in front of you. They battle amongst themselves, compete for the food you've put in. I like to think that this competition increases confidence, that the fishes natural wariness and caution is lessened, making them more likely to accept the bait with the hook in it.

All of this is pointless if you aren't fishing where you've accurately set the depth, and fed where you want the fish to be. You have to be quite pedantic about it, if you're going to get it right.

Initially, I feed every cast. Maybe only a pinch of a few pellets or a few maggots, but I establish a habit – cast, feed, get a bite, land the fish, recast, feed etc etc. If there are small fish in front of me and I notice Rudd or similar intercepting bait at the surface, I might use some simple ground bait or breadcrumb to bind the feed into a fast sinking ball, get it down quickly; or I may just increase the feed rate, hoping some of it gets onto the bottom, where my hookbait is.

All of this applies to rivers just as much as stillwaters. The difference is, in a river, you have to work out exactly where your loosefeed is going. If you have 4 feet of fast water as your 'swim', it's pointless feeding in front of you. Maggots and casters, and even pellets, will take 15 or even 20 yards to reach the bottom because of the current. Feed upstream – a catapult is useful here – and try and get the bait to hit bottom at the same time your hookbait does, a few yards below you.

On stillwaters, it can sometimes pay to follow the Carp anglers' example and feed in bulk at the start of your session. Their technique is to feed heavily, and put down a 'bed' or 'carpet' of feed, hoping that bigger fish will move in and stay put. This approach can work well for Tench and Bream, and is worth trying. Groundbait can be laden with maggots, casters, chopped worm, sweetcorn, hempseed... everyone has their favourite mix.

Another thing worth thinking about is the actual position of your loosefeed in relation to your float, and the place you plumbed up at the start. This is a good tip – *always feed up an area just past, just beyond, your float.* Here's why...

Imagine this : Our accurate feeding has enticed a shoal of decent fish into the area. Lets assume there are mainly small Bream ('skimmers', they're called round here!), with a few decent Roach as well. We're catching a few, getting into a rhythm, catching, casting, feeding... Unbeknown to us, a good Tench has been attracted to the area, drawn in by the activity of the smaller fish. He starts to feed, physically moving smaller fish out of the way. Then he picks up our hookbait, the float wobbles and then slides under... (Perfect so far... that's what's supposed to happen...) Our strike sets the hook and the Tench is away, fighting hard like Tench do, until it slides gently into the landing net, our best fish of the session. After the fish is returned, we settle back into the routine... And never have another bite... a promising start turns into a poor day... obviously, the Tench is to blame, he's frightened off the other fish...

Hopefully a few readers are having a 'that's happened to me' experience at this point, but it isn't all the Tench's fault. We hooked the fish in the middle of our carpet of loosefeed, and then the larger fish careered around, scattering smaller fish, loosefeed, stirring up mud and silt, and all our hard work is ruined.

The trick is to feed an area just past where you're fishing, and pick off smaller fish from the edge of the feeding shoal. Hopefully it's removal from the 'pack' goes unnoticed by the rest and the area that you've fed remains undisturbed. When a bigger fish comes along, you encourage it to run *across* rather than *away,* so it doesn't run through the baited area. The battle can then take place elsewhere…

This obsession with accuracy isn't just restricted to float fishing, by the way; it applies to legering as well. Casting distances accurately isn't easy, but there are two things you can do to help. First is to line yourself up with a marker in the distance, like a tree or a fence post or something. That gives you a 'line'. The you have to hit the same distance every time along that line. This can be done with a line clip on the reel spool, which is fine if you aren't catching Carp, but a disaster if anything you hook tries to take line off you. An alternative is to tie in a tiny piece of rubber band, or coloured yarn or wool, or mark the line with a marker pen, to identify when the desired distance is reached. Overcast, then wind in until your marker is back on the spool.

You may think all this pedantry is completely over the top and unnecessary. If you're the sort of pleasure angler (and I have days like this!) who just wants to enjoy 'being there' and for whom the occasional fish is enough, then all of this isn't for you. If you want to catch more – this accuracy thing is just another aspect of doing it properly. It really does make a difference.

Bream and the Racetrack

I used to enjoy putting a keepnet full of Bream together, especially on venues like Willesley Lake, or on the Norfolk Broads on holiday. Usually I'd fish a groundbait feeder and use maggots or worms, and over a session twenty or so fish would give you a good weight. I always thought, as the day wore on, that a few bigger fish would make a difference, and would try a larger bait. It rarely worked; Bream shoals tend to be made up of fish of similar size, so if you were catching 'skimmers' about the 12oz mark, that's what you'd catch all day, if the shoal stayed in front of you.

Some Bream shoals are vast, containing literally thousands of fish. In some big rivers and larger canals and drains they can cover great distances. In Ireland, especially on the Erne system, I remember locals were able to track the shoals moving in and out of the Lough, and advise visiting anglers whether to head for the river, rather than the Lough itself.

If you found yourself in the middle of one of these massive shoals, you were in for a busy day, and would catch consistently until you had to pack up. More often, though, on the lakes and gravel pits of the Midlands, the bites would dry up as the shoal moved off. Later in the day, you'd start catching again; the shoal had returned.

I wondered about where they went. We're thinking about hundreds of fish, not a few. They take up a lot of room, occupy a large area. Putting loads of groundbait in would hold them for a while, but eventually the inevitable happened and the shoal would move away, only to return later on.

Recently I started enjoying a few visits to an old estate lake on the Staffs/Cheshire border. It's nearly a mile long and proportionally quite narrow at maybe 70 yards across, and our club has access to a single bank. The Carp lads throw their baits huge distances to inaccessible bays and weedbeds on the far side, whereas I tend to target lily beds and overhanging trees close in. I've done OK, picking up some Tench and some decent Roach, and then, for a change, I cast a 'feeder out about 25 yards and sat back to see what happened. The tip pulled round, I struck into something heavy, and a good Bream hit the net a few minutes later. It was like fishing Willesley Lake all over again, but 30 years further on. I had six or seven, all around the 3lb mark, and then, inevitably, it went quiet. Just before I packed up, the fish returned, and I had two more.

I've been back a few times, and have always managed to catch a couple. Some have been quite large (the locals reckon there are some double figure specimens around) but the problem is always the same - I can't catch consistently. The shoal moves off, only to return later. It's like they're moving around out of habit, almost as if there is somewhere they have to be, or had a schedule to keep. So where do these fish go? If I knew, I'd know where to cast. If I knew, I'd know where to throw in a stack of groundbait. But I didn't know, and it was starting to irritate.

I really gave this one some thought. It's often said that 'fish follow the wind' and they do, that's where a lot of food will be. I tried a session with the wind in my face and then again at the windward end of the lake, and the results were the same. I did notice though, that the slack period where the fish had moved away, was roughly the same length of time; say a couple of hours. Was that significant?

It took one more fairly random observation before the jigsaw sort of fell into place. I mentioned earlier that the lake was long and narrow in shape, and we fished one bank only. The opposite bank was part of the estate, and only a privileged few had access. It didn't matter, if you wanted to fish the far bank, a long cast with a heavy Carp outfit would get you there. My 25 or 30 yard cast with a feeder got me about a third of the way across. What eventually became obvious, was that when I was catching, the anglers opposite weren't. When they were, I wasn't…

I figured the Bream were moving up and down the lake, in a sort of racetrack or oval … As they passed me, I'd catch a few, then the bites dried up as the fish moved off. The anglers opposite me would have their turn as the same happened to them, and then they'd come back to me as the shoal patrolled past once more. The two hour gap I mentioned was the time it took to do a full circuit.

My next visit proved the point. I chose a spot in the middle of the bank, where I had plenty of open water in front of me, and cast to my right, about 45 degrees. (Imagine a clock face - that's halfway between 1 and 2 o'clock). I had to wait a while for the shoal to come round- a lap of the racetrack - but after half an hour I started to catch a few. The bites dried up, so I cast this time 45 degrees to my left, and caught immediately. I bagged three more, then the shoal moved away onto another lap, and I knew it would be a couple of hours before I could catch again away to my right. I did try throwing a big Arlesey bomb right across the lake to try and catch as they moved along the back straight... an epic failure! Light Avon rods aren't designed for that sort of cast.

So it would seem that Bream shoals move around, and they have a pattern or route, which I would think they only deviate from when spawning or if there's a flood or some other drastic change in depth. I wonder if they always move clockwise, like the shoal I described earlier?

Postscript: I've just sketched out some distances and angles, with my position on the bank as the centre of a circle. My drawing, and the calculations of angles, distances from the bank, etc, revealed something I hadn't previously appreciated. Most anglers, when Bream fishing, will 'clip up' their lines to the reel spool, effectively fishing with a fixed length of line, so they always cast the same distance. (This accuracy is vital if you're feeder fishing as it concentrates you bait in one spot, and the clipped up line doesn't matter if you're catching Bream because they don't fight as such; it's often said they put as much resistance as a wet sack. Hooking a Carp with a clipped up line is asking to be smashed up because you can't release any line when the fish runs away from you.) So if you clip up at 25 metres, but then cast 45 degrees to your right or left, you're no longer fishing 25m out from the bank – it's less. Until I worked it out, I didn't appreciate how much less. If you imagine yourself, sat on the bank, as the centre of a circle, your fixed length of line at 25m, when cast out straight in front of you, is effectively the radius of that circle. Now if you cast out 25m of line at your 45 degree angle, the point where your tackle lands is closer in, further round the circumference of the circle. At 25m radius, it's only 17.7m out from the bank. At 30m, it's only 21m out.

If the shoal you're targeting is occupying an imaginary racetrack only 3 or 4m wide, you're going to, potentially, miss them altogether…

Carp off the Top

Catching Carp, or even Chub or big Rudd, on freelined floating crust, is one of the most evocative methods there is. Everyone loves it. It's pure and simple, the antithesis of modern Carp fishing. The classic approach requires nothing more than an eyed hook tied directly to the reel line. It's easy to do, but to do it well, and successfully, you have to have an understanding of fish behaviour, especially about how they feed.

Firstly, while Carp appear to feed readily on the surface, I'm not convinced that a surface bait would be their preferred, or ideal, choice. Taking a lump of crust or biscuit off the top means that the fish may also ingest a quantity of air, which it subsequently has to get rid of. Trout would have a similar problem, but they have evolved a technique to avoid that happening. Carp haven't.

A classic Trout 'rise' isn't what it appears to be. The big swirl on the surface, as most fly fisherman will tell you, isn't usually a fish taking a fly off the top. An instant response will leave you striking at nothing. What the

Trout has done is sink the fly, drowning it. Seconds later it is sucked in with a mouthful of water, exactly as the fish has evolved to do. (Tradition, for some older dry fly anglers, dictated murmuring 'God Save the Queen' before striking. Personally, I count to three…!).

Our Carp, however, motivated by greed and the competition of other fish in the area, will suck in your crust off the top, making a characteristic slurping sound as they do so. After a while, surplus gas has to be expelled, and Carp do this by simply burping up bubbles, which float to the top.

Most of the time that Carp are feeding on the surface, they're after snails. They eat other floating things as well - I once spent a memorable afternoon watching a Carp suck blackberries off an overhanging bramble bush - but they do seem to have an affinity for simple, plain white bread. (So do Trout! An old poachers trick is to fish floating breadcrust on a handline…)

There are two ways to tackle surface feeding Carp - either at range, or close in. The range method involves using a simple bubble float or a modern controller, and the bait is cast out to the desired spot. The Carp will generally hook itself. This is the only technique if you want to catch near a distant weedbed or overhanging tree. Getting bread to stay on the hook during a cast like this, however, is a problem all of its own, and I'll mention that later on.

Close in work is proper, classic freelining. An eyed hook, say a size 10, tied direct to the reel line, is all you need. Lines of 5 or 6 lb breaking strain will be ideal for single figure fish, something a little heavier is needed for snaggy areas full of lilies and suchlike, or bigger fish. The rod needs to be quite soft, and an 11' Avon rod is ideal for the smaller fish. A 12' Carp rod with a test curve of about 2lb is good for the bigger fish or heavier lines. This close in approach has the added advantage of being able to 'stalk' your target fish, dropping your crust a few feet in front of a feeding fish. The excitement builds as the fish moves towards your bait, then turns to frustration as they decide to ignore it! This is not a technique for those with high blood pressure!

Before you start fishing, a good idea is to actually get the Carp feeding confidently. Just throwing a few bits of bread in as if you were feeding the ducks is better than nothing, but a few minutes observation first is worthwhile. Try and identify the wind direction, and the surface flow. The majority of the surface feeding fish in the lake will be tight into the downwind bank, feeding on the food items trapped in the surface film and blown there by the wind. If the bank has grass and reeds overhanging and resting on the surface so much the better, as this is where your free offerings will end up. Resist actually fishing for a while, and get the fish feeding confidently on the bread you put in. Ten minutes or so is usually long enough to get them preoccupied with your bread crusts. Dog biscuits, known as 'Mixer', are also a good idea. Soaked so they soften slightly, they are excellent as feed. My preferred approach, certainly this year, has been to feed Mixers and use bread on the hook. Mixer biscuits are cheap too - a big bag of supermarket own brand Mixer is a couple of pounds at most.

The best bread to use as bait is an old fashioned, uncut 'tin' loaf. Mass produced sliced bread may be cheaper, but it's that solid, hard crust we need. Look for the almost out of date stuff that's marked down in price, and leave it somewhere dry and airy, out of its bag, to go stale. Cutting it into thick slices on the bank will let you tear off a chunk of crust with a bit of the white flake still attached. The hook goes in through the crust and then out again, so the point is showing. The idea is that the crust floats flake side down, with the shank of the hook, and the line, projecting from the top, hidden from the Carp approaching from underneath. This method also means your crust has a chance of staying on the hook for longer, and also for a long cast.

While it's true that Carp take a surface bait straight down, unlike trout, it still pays to delay the strike by a second or two. Carp will suck the bait in, and then sink back down; they don't turn away with the bait. An upward strike will often pull the hook, sometimes with the crust still attached, straight back out of the fish's mouth. A strike sideways doesn't seem to work so well for me, either. My best results have come from delaying just that second or two.

Another technique, written about in many old books from the fifties and sixties, suggests dropping your crust on the edge of a lily bed and using the pads themselves to 'screen' the line, hiding it from the feeding fish. Allowing the crust to drift up tight to a lily pad will successfully hide the line completely. Now I've tried this, and it works, but I lose more fish than I land, as they bolt for the safety of the lily bed. Only when the occasional fish has run for open water have I landed it. There is a theory that if you pull the fish *towards* the lilies it will run in the opposite direction - into open water. This is counter-intuitive, and I haven't tried it yet.

There is no better way of catching Carp on a summers evening; it's exciting, simple, and rewarding. Any angler can utilise basic tackle and learn to do it well. I often wonder how many of today's Carp anglers, all of which will admit to enjoying 'catching 'off the top', have tried simply freelining crust under their rod tip or even closer?

The Crucian Carp

There used to be a small lake just outside Fazeley, near Tamworth, called 'Beresford's Pool'. I have no idea who Beresford was. The pool was about an acre in size, silted up, and surrounded by trees. One of our local clubs had the lease, and I loved the place.

Back in the 80's we'd fish the margins for small Carp and Tench, and there were Perch and Roach as well. One year, out of boredom, I threw a big waggler out into the middle, sprayed maggots with a catapult, and discovered that the previously unexplored centre of the pool was full of better Carp. They weren't huge, a 3 pound fish was a good one, but great fun on match tackle. What set this pool apart, though, was the other species present – Crucians.

I would think, given today's obsession with Carp and the need to bank a '20', that many anglers have never caught a Crucian. They aren't exactly huge; the current record is 4lb 10 oz. It's hard, though, to think of another fish that anglers have such affection for. Even a little one makes you smile!

A small, rounded, almost dumpy fish, Crucians are native to the UK and love small ponds and lakes, preferably muddy, silty ones. They breed fanatically, like Perch, and will oust other species by sheer weight of numbers. Sadly, a 'true' Crucian is becoming a rarity, as they readily interbreed and 'hybridise' with Carp and illegally introduced Goldfish. In fact, a true Crucian is now classed as an 'endangered' species.

I haven't caught a decent Crucian for many years; I remember a 2 lb fish from Shuttington Pool in 1985 or thereabouts; I was catching Bream at the time, the Crucian was a surprise. Remembering that fish, and the fun we had at Beresford's, reminded me why this species used to be so sought after. Small ones are easy; light tackle, small baits and hooks... but a big one is another proposition altogether. A 'big' Crucian is anything over a pound in weight...

If you could choose a single adjective to describe a Crucian it would be 'finicky'. Or just plain 'difficult'. A Crucian will toy with a bait, play with it, making the float dip and move about, frustrating the angler until impatience wins and you strike at nothing.

One of the reasons I joined my current club was because of a small pool that reminded me so much of 'Beresford's'. It's old, silted up, and has lots of Crucians in it, amongst some Carp and Tench. As usual, all of the locals had tales to tell of enormous Carp… but some of them spoke, almost wistfully, about good sized Crucians, and how special they were. Obviously, I had to try and catch one.

As I said earlier, small ones are easy. Light float tackle, 16 or 18 hook, light lines and a single maggot or small pellet, or even sweetcorn, will get you a fish a cast if you feed correctly. I fished the pool several times, and caught lots, but I never managed one above about 4 or 5 ounces, say 6 to 8 inches long. If I tried a bigger bait, I caught Tench, or Carp, which usually smashed everything up because I was fishing so fine. So here was a problem to solve. How could I find a bigger one?

I really gave this some thought. Trying a bigger bait might have worked eventually, more by accident than design. But to catch my big Crucian, I really needed to stay with fine tackle, only slightly heavier than I'd used on the small ones. Putting a big bait, to avoid the small fish, on light line and hooks is asking for trouble. I had to stay fine, had to use small baits.

In the end I decided simply to keep feeding, hoping to fill up the small ones and attract the bigger fish, waiting for the small stuff to move away. This was going to take an age, because of the huge number of small Crucians in the pool, but I hoped that eventually that the smaller fish would simply move off, allowing the bigger fish to feed on uninterrupted.

It was going to be a long day! I lost count of the small, 2 to 3 ounce fish I caught. Eventually I caught some that were so full of maggots and pellets their mouths were full and their bellies bloated. I kept feeding, caught some small Tench, got broken by a Carp. Finally, patience was rewarded. My decent Crucian lay in the mesh of the net, well over a pound in weight … an old, battle scarred, tatty looking fish, but special nonetheless.

I didn't bother to weigh it - these days I rarely do. It wouldn't have made 2 pounds, it was probably just over 1 and a half, but that wasn't important. I've just heard that another of our club pools has produced - allegedly - a 3 pound fish, so that's my next Crucian target!

Trout Fishing

Bungs... not the financial kind

And you thought a bung was something allegedly given to a football manager...

Wandering around my local trout lake recently, most of the regulars were using one, of one form or another. Some were almost embarrassed about doing so! Talking to everyone made me realise what an emotive subject the bung is in flyfishing... so what is it, where does it come from and why does it work? And why is it so controversial?

The 'bung' is also known as a 'strike indicator'. It's a polystyrene ball or similar that is attached to the leader above the fly. The angler watches the bung in the same way a coarse angler watches a float; when it sinks, you strike. Most bungs are brightly coloured, although a black one can work well under certain light conditions.

Some fly fishermen refuse point blank to even acknowledge the existence of the method, claiming it is almost coarse fishing. There are others who wouldn't go fishing without one, both on rivers and stillwaters.

Time for a few myths to be exploded... first of all, using a floating indicator of some sort to show a 'take' isn't new or revolutionary. It's been around for literally centuries, even amongst the purists on our rivers and lochs, who simply put a big dry fly on a dropper and used that to spot the take.

It is, without a doubt, hugely effective. Takes are spotted and reacted to before any indication reaches your hand, and in most cases before the line moves to any degree. You begin to spot takes that, were you fishing without a bung, you wouldn't have seen at all. Ultimately, it puts more fish on the bank.

This early detection is good news. More often than not fish are lightly hooked in the top lip, especially with buzzers. This makes them easy to unhook and release, often without the need to remove the fish from the water completely.

There is another reason why the bung is so successful, apart from visually helping the angler to detect a take. Imagine casting a team of buzzers or nymphs out across the wind on your favourite lake. The gentle breeze pushes the floating line around in a graceful curve, which in turn pulls the flies through the water behind. Picture what is going on subsurface. As the team drifts round, the flies are constantly, slowly and deliberately, sinking. You may hit a fish half way through the drift on several occasions and reason that that is where the fish are. In reality, the fish may be widely scattered, it's simply that at that point in the drift, your nymph is at the right depth. 30 seconds later, it has sunk another foot, and is underneath the waiting fish.

The bung allows the angler to alter the depth at which his flies are fished *for the duration of the drift.* Find the taking depth, and you put your flies in the 'kill zone' for almost the entire cast. This gives you an enormous advantage, making you fish more efficiently.

A further advantage can be gained from fishing a bung in a good ripple or wave. As the bung rises and falls on the swell, the fly rises and falls as well, moving almost vertically in the water. This vertical movement is possible using other techniques (the 'washing line' is one), but cannot be achieved with a 'normal' retrieve. This vertical movement is deadly – mainly because it's an accurate representation of the behaviour of the natural bloodworm, a major component of the trout's diet all year round.

Now theres a thought. Flyfishing, for the purists amongst us - (I understand this, by the way – I would rather catch one trout on a buzzer than 5 on an orange blob) – is about imitating, accurately, the trout's natural food. How is fishing a good bloodworm pattern, under a bung, rising and falling naturally, different from fishing a dry hawthorn fly during a fall of naturals?

The beauty of this wonderful sport is in it's diversity. There is something there for everyone, from all walks of life, from all social backgrounds, from both sides of the proverbial fence. I admire the purists, the traditionalists, the anglers who maintain the methods and ideals from years ago. I understand the anglers for whom a day by the waterside is about the wildlife, the tranquillity, the company of other fishermen rather than the fish they catch. I can also appreciate the forward thinking, experimental type of angler that tries new techniques, new fly tying materials, new ideas.

The controversy surrounding 'The Bung' will be around for a long time. If it appeals to you, try it. If it doesn't, don't!! But whether you agree with the method or not, remember we are all, as Izaak Walton wrote, 'brothers of the angle'. We're all still fishermen, whether we use a Bung or not!

Emergers... Rises that are not what they appear to be!

If I had to choose a favourite flyfishing method, I'd probably choose the technique I'm about to describe. Before I go into detail, I'll tell you a story ...

Many years ago I used to fish a small trout fishery deep in the Staffordshire countryside that was known as an 'easy' water. The owner made sure there were plenty of stock fish and, if you'd promised a neighbour a Trout for their supper, you were sure you'd deliver.

I'd arrived after work and took my time setting up; the usual chat to other anglers, tea from the Thermos, swap a few flies, sample some Sloe Gin from someones hip flask. No rush. The days anglers were packing up, heading home with their limits and the usual tales of monster trout, smashed leaders, missed takes and excuses. Confidently, my tackle was assembled, 6wt outfit, floating line (a new Snowbee XS if memory serves), tapered leader down to a 5lb point. Fly of choice was a pheasant tail nymph, I didn't bother with a dropper. I think I started fishing about 6pm, with the lake to myself, planning on 2 quick fish, and time for a pint on the way home.

By 6.30pm I'd changed flies about 10 times and not had a take.

By 7pm I'd missed a good take and was becoming frustrated.

Just after 7pm the surface of the lake erupted, with rising fish everywhere. No more takes were forthcoming.

For the next hour I tried every dry fly in the box and even a size 20 Black Gnat was ignored. Some of my flies looked so realistic even the Swallows and Martins were having a look. The trout were hammering something, leaving huge swirls on the surface, and nothing I tried had any effect. In desperation I tried a bright, gaudy lure, and unfortunately foul hooked a 3lb fish, which shed the hook at the net. I had never been so frustrated... The fish were feeding avidly and everything I tried, failed.

With only half an hour to go before dark, I tied on a small Grey Duster, chosen mainly because I could see it in the poor light. A poor cast (tired arm!) splashed the fly onto the surface, whereupon it promptly sank. Before I could lift the rod to recast, the line tightened, and 2 minutes later a nice fish was in the net.

(The experienced amongst you will be smiling now, pleased that you sussed this out 3 paragraphs ago.)

I caught several more on the drowned, sunken Duster before I had to pack up, and it took me a while to work out what was happening. In fact, I think the answer came to me half way down a pint of Marston's Pedigree...

The answer, as I realised later, was that the fish were feeding not on the adult insect, or a terrestrial like a Hawthorn fly, or snails, or any other food item that Trout are known to become preoccupied with. They weren't feeding on a dry, or surface based, item at all. They were taking *Emergers,* fractionally under or in the surface film, and the swirl I'd seen wasn't a 'rise' at all.

While Trout (and other fish) feed on a varied diet, the one constant food item, all over the world, is the larvae of the Midge. This family of insects, known as *chironomids,* is huge. There are over 5000 species, including, mosquitos, sand flies, no-see-ums, and the infamous

Scottish Midge. All lay their eggs in water (even in a puddle if it's there long enough) and the larvae hatch out soon after. These larvae, known colloquially as a Bloodworm, are typically 3/8 inch long, red in colour, and thrash about in the mud and ooze on the lake bed. Some species ascend to the surface to breathe, but most live near the bottom and breathe anaerobically. The bloodworm is a protein rich, easy meal for a trout, and they will eat hundreds at a time. When the larva pupates, (into what the fly fisherman calls a 'buzzer'), it stops moving, and floats slowly to the surface, where it gets trapped in the surface film. The Adult insect hatches out of the pupa, fights it's way through the surface, and flies away.

While the pupa is trapped in the surface film, they are easy prey for a hungry Trout. The fish will either swirl at the emerging insect, drowning it before taking it, or simply suck it down from underneath. Both will leave disturbance on the surface, seen by the angler as a 'rise', and leading to the assumption that a fly has been taken off the surface, when in fact, all the activity was going on under the water, not on it.

The challenge to the angler is to imitate this. The larval and pupa stages are easy to imitate, bloodworm patterns exist for the larvae and there are many variations on the pupal stage with the ubiquitous 'Buzzer' tyings. What we have to do is suspend a buzzer pupa under the surface film, so it appears to hang there.

Originally this was achieved with a cube of foam tied in at the eye. It floated, and suspended the fly as required. A later, and I think better, variation arrived with the discovery of CDC feathers. A plume of these small, grey feathers worked well tied in at the eye, and could be dried out with a few false casts. (CDC is an abbreviation for the French 'Cul de Canard', literally a 'duck's arse'! They are naturally oily feathers taken from around the preen gland).

To fish these emerger patterns, a single fly is usually enough, cast into an area where a few 'rises' have been seen, and allowed to drift naturally. A gentle breeze is helpful, and make sure the leader itself has sunk, degreasing it if you need to. Takes are usually positive, and easy to hit. Sometimes it helps to fish a tiny nymph on a dropper to sink the leader; I think of the nymph as sacrificial, almost as a weight, but have caught on it occasionally!

To return to my earlier tale – having bought some emerger patterns I went back to the lake a few evenings later, full of enthusiasm. Not a single fish moved all evening and I went home (via the pub) fishless. Typical…

Autumn – Time to Target Fry Feeders

Autumn is almost upon us and for many fly fishermen this is the time to dust off the kit that has lain fallow all summer, and start thinking about getting back into things.

September and October can provide excellent sport but you do need to keep an eye on the weather. It can be notoriously unpredictable and you need to keep an eye on the changes and plan your approach accordingly.

The big issue at this time of year on most UK stillwaters is water temperature. It needs to drop following the heat of July and August, raising the oxygen level as a consequence and triggering a feeding response from the trout. The falling temperature is a sort of warning that winter isn't far away, and a signal to the trout to start putting weight on. And that means feeding on fry…

By now, this years coarse fish fry (predominately roach, bream and perch) will be about an inch long, and are abundant. That isn't to say a trout won't feed on other things – buzzers can still feature into October, especially if it's mild – but the fry will form the bulk of the trout's diet.

Generally, it's easy to find a fry feeder to cast at. Often, trout will smash bodily into a fry shoal, killing or stunning dozens at a time, returning to take them later. They will also follow larger fry, chasing them towards the surface. In both cases, feeding can occur very close in, as the fry will seek sanctuary in reedbeds, rushes and so on. Reservoir anglers faced with hundreds of acres of open water should watch for feeding gulls, taking dead fry from the surface; the trout won't be far away.

There are two main ways to tackle fry feeders, depending what you think you have in front of you. If the fish are visibly taking dead or injured fry from the surface, then these are what you should target, and I'll look at how in a moment. If you think the trout are feeding at depth, then this is the time to dust off the sinking lines, and for some anglers this is the only time of the year they are used.

By changing between intermediate, sink tip and sinking lines of varying densities, different leader lengths, weighted flies and speeds of retrieve it is possible to control the depth you are fishing at very accurately. It helps tremendously if you actually know the depth of water in front of you, and the bailiff or fishery manager should be able to tell you to within a few feet.

Personally, I'd prefer to fish a sink tip and control my depth with leader length and speed of retrieve, counting my flies down an extra 5 seconds every cast until I get takes. This becomes impractical in deep water, however, and this is where the fast sinkers come into play.

Takes can vary between quite savage hits to more subtle nips and pulls, especially if you are using a pattern with a long tail. If you are getting lots of missed takes, try trimming the tail down a bit, usually the trout will be nipping at the tail of the fly and missing the hook altogether. Watch out as well for takes 'on the drop', while you are counting down to a depth.

Classic patterns for this style of fishing are the Appetiser and Missionary, both of which imitate roach fry. The Dog Nobbler, Nomad and especially the ubiquitous Cats Whisker, also come into their own in Autumn. Recently more specialist 'close copy' patterns have been popular, and these are often worth a try. Some traditional flies can also be successful, particularly the Silver Invicta and the Teal, Blue and Silver, which was originally conceived as a sea trout fly. However, the older styles lack the movement and liveliness provided by the marabou tails of the newer flies, and it is this movement that usually seduces the trout into taking.

The actual retrieve with these patterns is best varied, from a slow figure-of-eight to a fast strip. A good technique is to alternate between a long, slow, continuous pull followed by a pause. This allows the fly to sink between pulls, and is similar to the way a pike fisherman would retrieve a deadbait 'sink and draw'. Again, takes will often come as the fly sinks, 'on the drop'.

Fishing lures like this will sometimes result in what is usually called a 'follow', when a trout chases the fly in, turning away at the last minute. This can be incredibly frustrating for the angler, and opinion is often divided on the best way to turn these follows into takes. Do you stop, slow down, or speed up? All three have been known to work, by stopping you encourage the fish to practically swim into the fly, slowing down has a similar effect, and speeding up fools the trout into thinking his meal is escaping, provoking a take. I think the important thing is to do something different as your retrieve nears completion, sometimes just subtly changing direction can help.

The surface feeders, taking the fry from the top, require a different approach. The idea is to fish a 'floating fry' pattern, usually tied from foam or spun deer hair, on a floating line, exactly like you would a classic dry fly in May. You cast into the area where the trout has been feeding, and allow it to dead drift, imitating a stunned or dead fry. Takes are surprisingly gentle and usually easy to hit.

Keep an eye on the weather – the first cooler days of September can signify the resurgence of good trout fishing on your local stillwater!

Your first time

As I write this, the evening meal is finished, the kitchen tidy (ish) and Her Ladyship is recumbent in front of the telly, watching Westenders or whatever it's called. This is good news. I sit contentedly in the kitchen, with the remains of a bottle of red, some cheese, Pink Floyd on the ipod, and Her Ladyship is totally oblivious to the fact that I'm scribbling this and plotting my next fishing trip. Marvellous.

The next fishing trip is the subject of this article. Tomorrow, I'm going to a Trout fishery that I haven't visited for over 20 years. I've been thinking about my previous visits, remembering the successes (few) and failures (many).

What has occurred to me though, is that the lake I remember so clearly…well, it doesn't exist any more. Twenty years does a lot to a lake. What is the point in remembering all the things that worked, years ago? The lake I arrive at tomorrow may well be unrecognisable.

It will be shallower, for a start. All that silt. The weedbeds may well be bigger, the margins no longer as accessible. The Hawthorn hedges, a source of huge numbers of Hawthorn flies years ago, may no longer be there. The screen of Rowan and Crab Apple saplings along the one end will no longer be saplings, if they're still there all of that end of the lake will be in shade. Stocking policies will be different. The lake may have been modified – enlarged, deepened or whatever.

So when I get there tomorrow, all keen and enthusiastic, what should I do? What should *you* do when you arrive at a venue for the first time? What can we do to maximise our chances of putting fish on the bank and avoid putting 'nil' on the catch return?

For me, there are 5 things I can do that can give me an advantage. They are:

1. Talk to the Fishery Manager or Bailiff

Fact - Fishery managers want you to catch. I know – I used to be one. It's in their interest for you to go home with a limit bag and good things to say about their fishery. Fish taken means they turn their stock over and a regular restocking means lots of stock fish, and happy regulars. You going to your local tackle shop / pub and talking about your good day will encourage more anglers to visit. So – your first job is to seek out the boss and ask, "if you were fishing today, what would you do?"

2. Read the catch returns

Take these with a pinch of salt, not everyone is honest. But if the last ten anglers all claim to have caught on a black buzzer then that is probably a good fly to start with!

3. Talk to the regulars

Now, I'm not suggesting you make a nuisance of yourself here and become a pain. But I've never met an angler yet that would begrudge you a polite 'good morning' followed by an enquiring 'any good?'. If they're catching, or getting takes, they'll tell you… and that information could save you hours of effort.

4. Follow the wind

The wind can be your friend… and, from a casting perspective, your enemy! The fact is that the wind will push the top six inches of water (the 'surface layer') along until it hits the downwind bank, when it's turned over to create an undertow. The fish will follow this moving surface layer, feeding on the insect life trapped within, especially buzzers and terrestrials. Position yourself near the downwind end of the lake, then you know you'll have fish in front of you, some of which will be near the surface.

5. Get the basics right

Do the simple things well. Make sure your floating line is clean and straightened so it floats well and in a straight line. Degrease your leader so it sinks. Stick to a single fly if you aren't confident about droppers. Use a buzzer or a bloodworm. Cast across the wind, distance isn't important. Let the wind work for you, pushing the line along the surface in an even, graceful curve, pulling the flies along behind, as naturally as possible. Don't retrieve, just take up the slack.

With the exception of the catch return suggestion, all the above work for coarse fisheries as well, especially the bit about the wind. I would add, for the coarse angler, to always plumb the depth and fish on or near the bottom, but that's another article!

Postscript...

Well, I've returned to writing this a few days after my trip. I did as I've suggested above. The lake had changed, it had matured nicely but was still recognisable as the place I visited years ago. The management and the regulars were helpful and keen to see me do well. There was space at the downwind end, where the lake narrows, and I drifted two buzzers on the breeze, watching the line for takes. I had two fish in the first ten minutes – then nothing else! Why I didn't catch any more, and what I did to try and catch, is for another day!

Give a Dry a Try

Wandering around the trout lake one evening last week, it was good to see a hatch of small black midges coming off and rise after rise dimpling the surface. The trout were intercepting the hatching insects and taking them from within the surface film, or occasionally from the surface itself.

It's difficult to determine which is actually happening, but initially it is enough for the angler to accept that the fish are 'looking up' for their meal. You can then experiment with different patterns, trying emergers, dries, sunken dries and so on until you get a result.

I'll return to the actual technique in a moment, but before I do we need to go back to my wander around the other evening. We had 9 anglers around the lake, all seemed happy and they all commented on how good it was to see fish rising freely.

So far so good. But it was noticeable that none of them were fishing imitatively – five were fishing intermediate lines with lures or big damsels, the other four were on floaters, 2 fishing buzzers about 3 feet down and the others pulling nymphs in. Fish were being caught, and as I said, they all seemed happy enough.

I couldn't help but wonder why. Why position your fly several feet below where the fish were obviously feeding? So I went around again and asked, and the biggest problem appeared to be a lack of confidence in fishing a dry or emerger. One angler, whom I know well as a regular, who casts a good line and catches more than his fair share throughout the year, admitted to being unhappy unless he was "doing something", ie: physically moving the fly. He wasn't keen on fishing static, which you need to do with a dry pattern.

This confidence issue isn't unusual in fly fishing. It's particularly common when using buzzer imitations, which I'll cover in another article. So is this lack of confidence justified with dry fly tactics? I don't think so – it's a very simple technique – anglers just need encouraging to try it.

Dry flies either sit *on* the surface (typical dry fly) or *in* the surface film (an emerger pattern). Either way, the technique is simply to cast (with a floating line) to the area where a fish has been rising and wait for him to come back and have another go. The tricky bit is keeping the fly afloat, and, crucially, making sure the leader has sunk. Most anglers are aware of this but many struggle to achieve it.

Firstly, the fly itself. For many years the popular way to keep a dry on the surface was to treat the hackle with a silicon based gel like Gink. This is still an excellent method and it works well – you can even experiment with treating just part of the fly, encouraging part of it to dip into the surface film, creating an emerger. The golden rule with anything silicon, however, is not to get it onto your leader. If you do, it'll float on the top like a length of rope and be visible to any rising fish. Silicon has one other drawback as well – you can't use it with CDC patterns. 'Cul de Canard' or CDC, is the feather from the preen gland of a duck. Its is naturally greasy, and floats extremely well. It can be used to create hackles in dry flies, or as a wing for an emerger pattern, especially a buzzer. But silicon destroys the natural oils and should be avoided when using CDC. Incidentally, the main problem with CDC dries is cost – it's an expensive material – and commercial tyers, in my opinion, rarely use enough of it.

There are other floatants on the market other than the silicon gels. I'm not keen on the aerosol sprays as I find them wasteful and difficult to apply accurately. A good product, and one you can use on CDC, is dessicant powder, like the 'Top Ride' made by Loon. This removes moisture from the fly, and, combined with a couple of vigorous false casts, should return the fly to a floating condition.

The leader is our second area of concern and, unlike the flies, we actually want this to sink. It needs to be subsurface to avoid detection, but not sink so efficiently it pulls the fly under. The original 'Ledasink' invented by the late Richard Walker in the 60's, is still available. You can make your own, from a putty made from Fullers Earth powder, washing up liquid and a drop or two of glycerine. (Fullers Earth is harder to get these days, as chemists no longer stock it as powder, only as a cream. My last packet came from a vet!) At a push, some mud will do, especially if it has some grit in it. All these sinkants work by degreasing the leader and roughening it's surface, helping it broach the surface tension.

So, floating line, degreased leader, size 16 CDC black gnat, drop it neatly where a few trout are rising... and wait... the only movement you want is the natural drift.

Give a dry a try next time you have rising fish in front of you... have confidence, and some very rewarding sport can be yours.

How many Flies?

What's you favourite fly? Flies are to a Trout or Salmon fisherman what floats are to a coarse angler. Everyone has a favourite, and we can't resist collecting new versions, or different colours, or sizes, or whatever. For me, 'My Fly' is a simple black or red buzzer, tied in the modern style, with clear epoxy over a flexi floss rib.

Some seasons ago I sorted out my flyboxes and had a proper look at what 25 plus years of fly fishing does to a fly collection. It was a mess, and I discovered flies in old boxes I'd forgotten about. I was well overdue a 'sort-out'…

A group of us were discussing this one evening when nothing was being caught and the bar at The Old Crown was becoming an attractive alternative proposition. Bob Sanders suggested organising flies into groups, perhaps with a box for each. I found that interesting, coming from Bob; I always describe him as a 'fly-dresser' rather than a 'fly-tyer', as some of his creations defy classification and are rarely alike. We settled on four groups - Buzzers, Nymphs, Dries and Lures. (I know some people think of buzzers as nymphs, but you get the idea.)

A proper debate followed about fly boxes. I favoured 4 smallish ones, to fit in the pockets of my fly vest, as I don't carry a bag. Bob favours a bag, and therefore wasn't concerned about the size of the boxes. He has quite a collection, including some beautifully made, and expensive, Richard Wheatley ones that looked amazing. After studying numerous catalogues we eventually settled on a plastic box called a Theseus. I think we ordered 4 and got 4 free, or something like that. They weren't expensive, and are functional rather than flashy, and my final point in the argument settled it. "Drop that in the water" I said, pointing at £70-worth of hand built brushed aluminium flybox, "and it'll sink like a stone - you'll lose the lot!". Plastic boxes - they float!

So we went with plastic. It was then that the 'what's your favourite fly' conversation really got started. Bloodworm? Pheasant Tail? I spoke about my biggest Brownie, taken from Danebridge on a tatty old Damsel pattern that I still have, and which sits reverently in a corner of a box as a source of inspiration. Then, predictably, I mentioned buzzers and was promptly told to be quiet. Bob talked about a stonefly pattern he created which accounted for some big Irish trout. Loz Watton spoke in hushed, awed tones of an old pattern called a Docken Grub; it's a sort of fat, creamy coloured buzzer. I said it looked like a maggot. Anyway. The discussion continued for ages, like it does amongst fishermen the world over.

I stick by my choice of a simple black buzzer though. I rarely use much else, to be honest. A buzzer pattern can do it all, all year round. You can fish it static, or pulled, albeit very slowly. You can fish it deep, or shallow, or as an emerger. There are innumerable sizes and colours to choose from, and scores of different materials used to create different profiles and silhouettes. And it's imitating the most natural food of all - the midge pupa, of which a trout will eat literally millions in its lifetime.

Giving this favourite fly thing some more thought, I wondered... if the buzzer was my favourite, the fly I used the most... then why have I got boxes filled with literally hundreds of flies, ranging from big, garish lures to size 18 black gnat? How many flies do you actually *need?*

I found an old, empty fly box and over the months that followed I used it to store 'used' flies, a bit like a traditional river fly fisherman would use a 'drying box' with air holes in to dry out delicate dry flies. After a while I filled the box, so I examined the contents. I found that I'd used lots of flies, but essentially, only 5 generic patterns. They were:

Buzzer, Bloodworm, Damsel, Hopper, and Pheasant Tail nymph.

Now, I hadn't fished during the winter when I made that list, so I would almost certainly add a marabou tailed, fry-imitating lure pattern like a Cats Whisker to the list. The point is, though, that that still only total six patterns. Even with a few variations for colour, hook size etc., why do I need 4 boxes full?

Sink your Leader!!

Ever wondered why the angler next to you is having fish after fish, while you can't buy a take?

Ever wondered why what could be your best fish for ages (or even a lifetime) rises confidently to your fly, only turning away the last minute?

Ever wondered, simply, *why?*

A few moments of intense thought (and I do a lot of this intense thinking; it fills the gaps and spaces, the times when I'm not catching) will lead to an inevitable conclusion. It has to be the leader. The fly did its job. The fish was prepared to take it, turning away the last minute. In a river when the fly is moving with the current a Trout has not got time to examine that fly in detail before accepting it. It has to be taken quickly or the current will take it away. In a Stillwater too even a dry fly is never truly static, there is always some movement. If a Trout rises to your fly he's accepted it... so what is the problem with the leader?

Basically, the trout has seen it. It looks unnatural. Self preservation overrides hunger and the Trout turns away, wary. You've got to hide the leader, make it invisible.

To do this, you have to make it sink.

Imagine a length of rope or string floating on the surface of a swimming pool. Imagine you dive in, swim underneath the floating rope, and look up just like a trout would. The rope looks huge. It's in shadow, for one thing, in silhouette against the sky above. It's also magnified by the surface film. Your leader, proportionally, appears similar to the rope. Sink the leader and the Trout can't see it ... It's that simple.

How hard can it be? All the books will tell you to give the fly line a sharp tug, break the surface tension, get the leader sunk. An excellent idea as long as the fly is designed to sink in the first place. What if it's a dry fly or emerger? You can certainly straighten the leader, take up the slack. Good idea. When you strike you have a better chance of successful hook up, a more direct contact with the fish. But a good 'tug' on the leader will sink the fly as well, and if we're using a dry or an emerger, that's the last thing we need. You can degrease the leader using a sinkant, either shop bought, or a homemade one, but you still have to give the line a 'tug' to get it to sink if you're using a dry fly or emerger.

In all fishing, doing the simple things well makes a huge difference, and controlling the behaviour of your leader is no exception. You have to get the leader sunk, while the fly floats.

You need to look at the material the leader is made of. Today you have 4 choices: Nylon, pre-stretched Nylon, Fluorocarbon, and Copolymer.

Nylon is the first choice of many; it's cheap, readily available, has excellent knot strength. Sadly unless we treat it in some way it's natural tendency is to float, not a desirable characteristic. Pre-stretched nylon has similar issues; despite the fact that stretching makes it considerably thinner (Its smaller cross section can cut through the surface film more easily) it still has a natural tendency to float. Normal nylon also has a bit of 'give' in it, it will stretch when you're playing a fish, which is useful. Pre-stretching obviously removes this. I think it's true to say that a thinner diameter would get you more takes, but I don't like the way it feels; somehow more fragile. I'm not convinced that the pre-stretched stuff makes good knots either, for the same reason. It feels brittle, almost; and if I've no confidence in it, it goes in the bin!

Copolymer has a separate issue ; It costs a fortune! Its known for its suppleness, which can make a huge difference to presentation, but I struggle to see past the expense. In comparing prices I was at first surprised to see copolymer priced similarly to fluorocarbon, until I realised that Fluo was a 100m spool and Coploymer was 30m! Recently, Coploymer has come down in price, but it's still comparatively expensive.

That leaves us with Fluorocarbon. Yes it's expensive compared to nylon, but not as expensive as copolymer. It sinks naturally as long as you can broach the surface film, has good knot strength and a very good breaking strain to diameter ratio. It's readily available, every tackle shop sells it as is it also marketed as a carp anglers rig material. Most importantly it has the same refractive index as water... now before the phone starts ringing with readers asking what refractive index is, I'll explain. It's important…

Any GCSE Physics student will tell you, Refractive Index is a way of measuring how a substance affects light. You know how if you look through a dirty window the image is blurry and distorted? That's because the dirty glass has a poor refractive index, the light passes through it inefficiently. Contrast that to clear glass or plastic, which has a better RI. Physics boffins compare substances to water to measure RI, some types of glass are actually better than water at refracting light, whereas some plastics are worse. Happily for us, Fluorocarbon has a similar refractive index to water, which means it's almost invisible, as long as it's sunk. By way of example Glass also has a similar refractive index to water; if you place a glass in a bowl of water it's almost disappeared… the same thing happens to your fluorocarbon leader.

The above example isn't perfect by any means, I'm sure a Trout's eyesight is far superior to that of a human, maybe they can still see the fluorocarbon, I don't know. What I do know is that I seem to get more takes with Fluorocarbon. I recall a trip some years ago, I think it was to Danebridge... I took Dad, and as usual I promised him a good day with plenty of fish. Despite us using the same method, same flies, I was on for fish after fish and the Aged One was struggling. We changed places, and the result was the same. When we swapped rods, though... I couldn't buy a take. The answer lay in the leader, it was the only thing different between the two set up's. I was using my usual Fluorocarbon, Dad was using a well known brand of pre-stretched nylon. We changed his leader, and he started to catch. To emphasise the point, I changed to nylon, and stopped catching.

I'm not suggesting you throw away all your old nylon, by the way... I'd keep some of the heavier stuff. A length of properly stiff, thick nylon, say 10 or 12lb breaking strain, makes a superb 'butt', efficiently bridging the gap between fly line and leader.

Try Something Different

I never cease to be amazed at the sheer variety and unpredictability of this wonderful sport. Every day brings something that makes you think, and one of the most valuable assets a fisherman can have is an open mind and a willingness to try new things.

For example, as I write this November is well under way and contemporary opinion says that the rainbows should be gorging themselves on fry in anticipation of a hard winter. Most of you will be nodding their heads in agreement at this point. November = Fry. Always has.

Except this year it isn't. Yesterday we were catching on buzzers, pheasant tail nymphs and black pennell. The sort of thing you usually associate with April. With the benefit of hindsight, it makes some sort of sense... it's so mild at the moment, it almost could be April, or September for that matter.

The point is that someone, at some point during his session yesterday, made a decision to throw away the rule book and try something different. I've written about this before, looking at how the fish don't actually know what time of year it is, and trying something 'unseasonal' sometimes works.

The culprit yesterday was Lichfield's Bob Sanders, whose flyboxes are a testament to trying something different. Bob scours his local shops for odd materials and finds unusual things to include in his fly dressings... I've always imagined that he occasionally approaches his neighbours' especially hairy dog with a pair of scissors hidden behind his back. He has been known to hold up traffic on a country lane while he cuts a section of skin and fur from a roadkill Badger lying in the road. His latest creation is a shrimp shellback made from cellophane from a Quality Street sweet wrapper. Ever seen a bright yellow shrimp before? Neither had I ... but it works...

It isn't just with flytying that thinking differently works, it applies to actual fishing as well. One freezing January day I watched an angler at Graiglwyd Springs catch fish after fish, and was convinced he was doing something illegal. I asked around and another angler told me he was renowned for catching lots of fish in the winter. On investigation, I found the angler was using a strike indicator to suspend his flies at depths of 2 feet (dropper) and 4 feet (point), and was fishing them static. Nothing unusual in that, but you would expect to find 2 delicate buzzers or similar tied to the leader. Not so … the home tied, marabou tailed creations being used – referred to simply as 'red things', or 'white things' or whatever colour combination appealed - were more akin to a dead budgie than any sort of aquatic food item. This sort of fly is supposed to work by retrieving at speed to impart movement and life to the fly… fished static they shouldn't work at all … but they do.

So why are so many anglers so set in their ways? One angler actually admitted to me – and this is verbatim - "I have a favourite fly I always use, I never use anything else". Later in the conversation he mentioned he was getting despondent because he rarely caught… Sometimes you have to try something different. I think we get obsessed with 'matching the hatch' or fishing imitatively, or trying a favourite lure, and I'm the biggest culprit of all, tying on my favourite red buzzer pattern out of habit and rarely thinking to try something else. Trout are also predatory; like Perch or Chub they will eat small fish, nymphs; I once found a fully grown Newt in the stomach of a 3 pound fish I caught at Thornton. One of these days I'm going to write 'No!' in marker pen on my buzzer box…

We're set in our ways because we stick with what we're good at; it's human nature. We find a sort of security or safety in doing something well, especially if it works and is successful. There really is a 'comfort zone', and as anglers we need to step outside it occasionally.

Postscript: Have just returned from a short session on a notoriously difficult stretch of the Blithe. It's weedy, overgrown, hard work. I bit off the hopper I usually use here and replaced it with a goldheaded bug - type thing with an garish orange hackle. I have no idea where I had it from, I suspect it might be one of Bob Sanders' experimental creations. I felt embarrassed, almost… I'm fishing a classic Staffordshire trout stream, and I'm using a fly that I'd think twice about using for stockie stillwater Rainbows. Well, it worked. Allowed to sink, and held so it bounced around in the current, it accounted for several small wild Brownies. The dry fly worked as well, but if I hadn't tried the bug I wouldn't have caught as many. I've often dropped a nymph pattern into a deeper hole and caught by twitching it back, but I've never fished 'static' before. In fact I can't find any reference of such a technique. Definitely one for further investigation - I may even try it with a fly with a marabou tail, allowing the current to move it about as I hold the fly static.

Trout don't know what month it is... it feels like September...

Back in the days when I was running fisheries, I would look forward to the occasional moment of quiet contemplation, the few minutes peace, quiet and tranquillity when I could take in surroundings and appreciate nature at its best. These moments were few and far between in the summer – there was always someone wanting something – but in winter, when it was quieter, it was essential to stop occasionally and 'take five'.

My mind still has a tendency to wander on these occasions, although these days it's usually when I'm not catching anything. Recently I was pondering during a breezy but unseasonably mild February afternoon. 'Feels like September', was my thought. Could be early October. My quiet five minutes was interrupted by a shout from along the bank, as a well meaning local enquired if I'd (quote) 'cetched owt?'. The rest of the day generated more food for thought...

February at most Midlands stillwaters, is fry bashing time. Those 'in the know' use small Minkies or Appetisers, and the Rainbows can be easy. Go a bit deeper and a Brown can be a welcome surprise. On the day in question, my quiet five minutes had been disturbed by an unhappy angler who, as usual, wanted to know if the lake had been stocked recently. (Typical – no takes in the first hour equals 'there's no fish in here' rather than 'what am I doing wrong?'). On this particular day, the Rainbows were far from easy. No one had caught all morning.

Now if I'm fishing, I actually enjoy days like this. It's a challenge. The fish have to feed, and if they aren't looking at a well presented Minkie or similar then their attention must be elsewhere. The trick, the skill even, is to find out where.

You can usually catch on a bloodworm or a black buzzer all year round – I know anglers that never fish anything else – and I suggested this as a Plan B to the frustrated, who changed flies immediately and tried again. By lunchtime, the result was the same – no fish.

There were no signs of fish moving, no obvious fall of terrestrials, not that after a February frost you'd expect one. Another attempt with lures proved fruitless and by 12.30 all the anglers were on the carpark drinking tea, contemplating opened flyboxes and seeking inspiration. The usual banter was replaced with a sort of quiet frustration. Any ideas anyone?

Gradually we all returned to the lake and tried again. My own idea was to fish a bloodworm deep and slow, needless to say I struggled. The wind got stronger, and the day became even more September-like. Suddenly, from along the bank, a cry of success and a 3lb fish on the bank for an old fishing buddy - Mark Robins. Mark has an enviable reputation as a wilderness angler, more at home on a tiny mountain stream than a 4 acre gravel pit. I knew he'd be fishing something imitative and returned to my bloodworm patterns with enthusiasm.

Ten minutes later he's had 2 more, and ten minutes after that he'd got an audience, as we all stopped fishing and went to watch. Here was a classic case of doing something differently, what the marketing types among you would call 'thinking outside the box'. Mark was using a goldhead Daddy, a daddy-long-legs pattern with a gold bead as a head, a 'drowned daddy' pattern usually associated with … wait for it … September. Minutes later we'd pinched all of Mark's spare Daddies and were catching ourselves.

Now, Mark maintains he tried the pattern simply out of boredom and the desire to try something unusual. There were no naturals about and the only thing that was 'right' about his choice of fly was the weather! So why did it work?

Well, anglers have always been aware of the time of year, and fly selection has always been influenced by the calendar. Certainly, it's a good indicator of where to start. Like I mentioned earlier, Daddies in September. Hawthorn Flies in May. Damsel nymphs in June. And so on. It's not that simple, though. Which is why I come back to why things work when they shouldn't.

Initially, I was thinking about colour. Trout don't see colours like we do; our eyes have things called 'rods' and 'cones' to split light up into colours so we can separate them, fish don't. They see, literally, in shades of black and white. So red, which is at one end of the spectrum, to fish, appears light grey. Purple (technically violet) appears almost black. I wondered if that's why, for me anyway, a red buzzer or bloodworm is so successful, because it shows up against a dark background? (Coarse anglers often favour red maggots as well).

However; no theory about colour can explain why some fly patterns work when they shouldn't. More thinking required. What about shape, or movement?

Now, I may be on to something. You can offer any fly you like to a Trout, at the right depth etc., but if it doesn't actually look edible, he isn't going to take it. I remember using a Montana nymph, years ago, and catching on it. A far more experienced fly fisherman than I pointed out, with some sarcasm, that the water must have had a terrific hatch of Stoneflies. It was much later that I understood his sarcasm – the Montana (clue in the name!) is an *American* fly pattern, based on a very large stonefly nymph. Such a thing has never existed in the UK… (actually we do have stoneflies over here, mainly in fast streams and rivers. Much smaller than their American cousins, some of which can be 2 inches long, 'our' nymphs look nothing like a Montana!). So, the Montana works because of what it looks like, and how it behaves in the water, not because of its colour.

Is it really that simple? Position something that looks like food at the right depth, as natural looking as possible (sunken leader!), and you catch your Trout!

Well, no. It's not that simple – and wouldn't it would be boring if it were?

Trout, remember, don't have a calendar to hand. They don't actually know it's September, or March, or whenever. Trying things that shouldn't work is a worthwhile exercise once in a while. We don't, for example, have a Mayfly hatch at any of my local stillwaters. (I wish we did). So why does a Mayfly nymph, fished slowly on a long leader, account for lots of fish every year?

Next time you are contemplating the contents of your flybox, hoping for a flash of inspiration that will turn a poor day into a memorable one, try something different. Try throwing away the calendar. If it feels like

September, pretend it is! Tie on that Daddy or that Hopper. The Trout will never know …

Miscellany

The One that Got Away

Cliches have their place; our language wouldn't be the same without them. 'The One that Got Away', 'It was THIS big', and so on. Angling writers are as guilty as anyone, and some angling cliches go back hundreds of years.

Reading fishing books, even ones by the great authors like Richard Walker, Chris Yates, Charles Rangeley-Wilson and co., you are always coming across articles that tell of lost fish, epic failures, the fish of a lifetime that got off. Am I alone in thinking I don't want to know about this? I want to read about the ones that 'graced the net' (cliche!), not the ones that didn't.

However! Giving it some thought, I wondered if this fallibility, this failure, was important after all. Do I need to know that the godlike Richard Walker, innovator, inventor, author, holder of the UK Carp record, occasionally lost a fish?

I have just consulted Her Ladyship on this one. She isn't an angler - horses are her thing. Back in her heyday, competing in Eventing, Show Jumping and Dressage, she said it was good to see Princess Anne end up in the water at Badminton, or see Mary King thrown off at Wembley or Olympia. It gave her hope - they weren't perfect.

I've just opened 'Walkers Pitch' at random and read about a big Carp he lost at Redmire in the 50's. Charles Rangeley-Wilson's 'Somewhere Else' is full of tales of lost monsters from Grayling to Trout to Tarpon and Bonefish. So now it's my turn…!

First up, and unusually for me, is a day trip sea fishing out of Gran Canaria in about 2002. The skipper spoke good English, there was about 10 of us on the boat of all nationalities, and there was talk of decent Tuna. The inevitable banter, in numerous languages, was entertaining and I knew that as the only Brit I was getting some stick. I retaliated by telling a Frenchman he stank of garlic. It was all good natured stuff, and there was much laughter. Apart from, the odd one out. Sorry to appear like I'm stereotyping - I'm not - but there was a 'fly in the ointment'… a German. He was taking this trip seriously, and didn't take part in the conversation.

Now, I've worked with a lot of Germans over the years; I actually worked for a German company many years ago. Without exception, they have all been the polar opposite of the stereotype. Anyway, we caught a few small Tuna, and the skipper moved us out over a deeper part of the Atlantic. Then, a shout from one of the Frenchmen and a good fish on. We all wound in and watched him go from cocky confidence to gibbering wreck in 10 minutes flat. Exhausted, he passed the rod to his compatriot. Less than 5 minutes later the skipper felt obliged to take the rod and feel for himself. His expression said it all - a big fish. He looked at his watch, shrugged his shoulders. We got the gist; this could be a while! The rod was passed around, eventually it was my turn, and I can say I have never felt anything like it. The fish felt heavy, powerful; nothing I did made a difference and after a respectable 10 minutes I handed the rod over to the next angler. Eventually, it was the German's turn. His body language said it all; he was going to beat this fish, show us all up, or die in the attempt! He accepted the rod, heaved... and made no difference. The fish, now being thought of by the skipper as the fish of a lifetime, kept straight on. The German tried again. In preparing to heave once more, he momentarily dropped the rod tip, giving a few feet of slack, and the hook, fell out.

I won't describe the trip back to port. Rather, I'll leave it to the readers' imagination. Suffice to say that the German was less than popular, and the hour it took to get us back was probably the longest of his life.

Here's another. As teenagers a group of us used to walk a mile or so to a stretch of the River Anker, run at the time by the Birmingham Anglers' Association. I've written before about the Anker; deep, fertile, weedy, full of fish. One summer we hit on a tactic to catch decent Perch, avoiding the gudgeon, baby roach and 'chublets'. We fished the margins, alongside lilies and reeds, well overdepth, with a few big AAA shot a few inches from the hook. The idea was to anchor a worm or bunch of maggots hard on the bottom in amongst all the roots and snags, where only a bigger fish would root it out. What we found was that all the big Roach and Chub were in the main flow, but the margins were full of Perch. By the end of the summer holiday a 1lb fish wasn't even worth mentioning, we'd caught lots. One day I hooked something bigger…

Perch have a recognisable 'fight', they jerk about a lot, and this fish plunged up and down with enthusiasm, making its way downstream at the same time. It accelerated, the line cutting through the surface with a sort of fizzing noise. Much to the amusement of my companions as I leaned forward to keep the line away from an overhanging bush, I fell in. As I stood up, dripping wet, the howls of laughter behind me died away as the fish turned and decided to run upstream instead. I kept the pressure on, and the float broke surface briefly as it went past. Younger brother Martin reckoned he could make out a shadow under the surface; it was huge, he said. A few seconds later the fish gave a determined and sudden 'tug', the line snapped just above the hook, and that was that. All I remember now, 30 -plus years later, is that it *felt* like a Perch. It could have been a Pike, but if it was a Perch, it was enormous.

To complete the set, so to speak, a tale of a lost Trout. I can still get quite upset about this one! One of my old fly fishing buddies, Mark Robins, was always raving about his favourite trout fishery in North Wales, near Wrexham. It was miles away and I always declined to go, only to hear him talk about it all the more. Eventually I gave in, and met him there. It's imitative stuff, he said. Lures no good. Small flies best. As the day wore on, and no-one caught, I was using flies that got smaller and smaller. I had a take on a tiny nymph, and missed it. Mark missed a rise to a small dry. As evening approached and more fish showed on the surface, I tied on a tiny size 18 Black Gnat, the smallest fly I had. The eye on the hook was so small I had to add a length of 3lb line as a tippet. Last cast of the day, big swirl, count to three, strike, fish on. So far, so good. Darkness crept up on us and the fish stayed out in the middle, circling. A small crowd gathered, including the bailiff, who wanted to lock up and go home. Opinions were offered freely … big Brownie? Blue Trout? The less charitable suggested it might be foul hooked. Finally, aided by the light from someone's car headlamps, I guided the fish towards the net, the Gnat just visible in its jaw. Positively identified now as a Rainbow trout well into double figures, and certainly the largest I've ever seen, let alone hooked, I reached forward with the net, the fish rolled, and the 3lb tippet parted like cotton as the weight of the fish bore upon it. I lunged with the net, missed, and the fish rolled upright. Exhausted, it gave a flick of its tail, and glided back into the depths. No-one said a word.

Three separate tales of abject failure! I can still see that Trout, if I close my eyes and daydream. It really was that big, and it was worse because I actually saw it. I've lost other fish, and I'll continue to do so, and I think it's important that I do. It's one of the things that makes us try harder, and go again, and keep on going. It fuels that drive, that desire; and that makes us better anglers. Plus it keeps those cliches alive! With that Trout, though, I can move my hands apart and say in all honesty, 'it really was THIS big!'.

The Resurgent River Tame

If you could choose an area in the UK to combine growing up and fishing, you'd probably choose somewhere like the Norfolk Broads, or somewhere similarly 'wet' and 'fishy'. A young fly fisherman may want to grow up in Hampshire near the river Test. Sea anglers would have a totally different outlook. For me, the south eastern corner of Staffordshire was perfect...

Tamworth could almost be an island there is so much water about. Three rivers, three canals, countless gravel pits, loads of farm ponds and pools. A short drive brought the rivers Trent, Dove, Sow and Blythe into range. Trout fisheries like Blithfield, Donkhill, Lloynton, Tittesworth and Gailey were all in Staffordshire. Commercial coarse fisheries sprung up everywhere. We really were spoilt for choice. (Sadly a lot of those Trout fisheries are now closed; only Blithfield and Lloynton are left).

In the 1970's however, there was a fly in the proverbial ointment. The mighty river Tame emerged from its birthplace in the industrial Black Country, called at

Birmingham, and arrived in Tamworth reeking of untreated sewage and devoid of life. The river that gave the town its name (in the middle ages, 'Tameworth' meant 'enclosure by the Tame'), was, as a river, practically dead. In fact, I recall being told it was Britains dirtiest river… I still remember that dirty, metallic tang… the Tame had a definite smell about it; it wasn't pleasant.

The river Anker meets the Tame in the town; the confluence being the reason people settled here in the first place. You couldn't find two more different lowland rivers. The Anker is deep, slow and fertile, and full of life. It is easier to list the fish species that *aren't* present. Some of the Roach were enormous. The Chub we caught were fat rather than lean and muscular. The Tame, by comparison, was wide, fast and shallow. Managed so that in places it was more like a canal or a Fenland drain, the Tame existed for one reason – to shift sewage and rainfall away from Birmingham as fast as possible. The river has a huge rate of discharge (measured at Hopwas, it averages 1000cuft/second – that would empty a 25m swimming pool in about 30 seconds) By the time it reaches Alrewas and the National Memorial Arboretum, its 35 metres across, dwarfing the River Trent that joins it just downstream. (It's interesting that the smaller of the two rivers – the Trent – gives its name to what follows, possibly because it is the longer of the two; normally, the larger, dominant river keeps its name downstream of a confluence.)

In the seventies and eighties, steps were being taken to clean the river up. A massive sewage treatment plant was set up at Water Orton, just north of the city. Rainwater was also being treated, by huge settlement and purification lakes at Lea Marston, and by the late 80's there were a few fish about, A local angling club had a stretch at Comberford. We used to catch small Chub next to an outflow from the water treatment plant at Coton. To be honest, as children our parents preferred us not to fish the river, as the smell lingered for days. The river still stank … and we never caught anything bigger than a few ounces.

Back in the autumn I bumped into an old mate, wildlife photographer Loz Watton. As well as being useful with a camera, Loz's fishing exploits are worthy of an article in their own right! He lives practically on the river, and knows the Tame as well as anyone. Our conversation, inevitably, turned to fishing and he commented that the river was 'fishing well'… not an observation I'd ever heard before! Loz spoke of lush weedbeds, prolific insect life, Kingfishers; he could have been describing a Hampshire chalk stream, not the open sewer I remembered from my youth.

Further investigation was called for and so I went for a walk, finding old footpaths that I last trod perhaps 30 years ago. The difference in the river I remembered was, well, remarkable. The water is clear, with large beds of streamer weed, and rushes growing in slack areas and cut outs in the banks. The river bed is hard, compacted gravel, washed clean of silt and dirt by the current. I saw Moorhens, Mallards, and the inevitable Canada Geese. Swans were common, (Tamworth did once have its own Swan Warden – Borrowpit Lake and the Castle Grounds supported a huge population years ago), and then I glimpsed a Kingfisher, electric blue flashing against a background of green. I actually saw several that afternoon, obviously thriving. A Grey Heron, motionless, stood as if on guard at the waters edge; I actually walked up to it before he took off, squawking.

Turning away from the river itself the woodland and hedgerows adjacent revealed more surprises. Buzzards mewed to each other as they soared overhead. A Kestrel hovered patiently, waiting for a vole or mouse to show itself. A pair of Yellowhammers, the first I'd seen for a long time, moved along the hedgerow in front of me as I walked. I saw more wildlife that afternoon than I had in years, all around Tamworth, Hopwas, and Elford.

The following day I walked across the ancient Ladybridge, in Tamworth town centre. You can see, upstream of the bridge, the confluence of the Anker and the Tame; downstream, the river Tame splits again into a separate flood channel, designed to protect the old Alders Paper Mill, which took its water from the river. The Environment Agency have installed a fish pass here, next to the weir, allowing spawning fish to head upstream. The Heron was again resident, perched on a rock next to the weir, feeding on small fish. Coots chased each other all over the river, and children fed scraps to dozens of ducks gathered at the waters' edge.

Obviously, I had to fish the river again, just to see. I caught some Chub, and a decent Perch; saw a good Pike move amongst the weed, waiting to pounce on some unsuspecting Roach.

As I write, Spring is well underway and the river is again coming back to life. The weed is back, long 'streamers' waving in the current. Marsh Marigolds, like massive buttercups, glow yellow in the sunlight. The smell of Ramsons - wild garlic- hangs in the air, competing with the more subtle aroma of Water-Mint. This once rancid, filthy watercourse is once again breathing life into this corner of our county, and I, and many other 'locals', are enjoying it very much.

If that's where the Tame is now, I wonder where it will be in 10 years time? There are Otters now as well, and the Kingfishers I saw are common along most of its length. Loz even has a photograph of a Little Egret stalking the now clean margins, not a species you'd expect to see this far north. And best of all, it doesn't smell anymore…!

The Fishing Club

Over my angling lifetime, I've been a member of many fishing clubs, varying from the enormous (the Birmingham Anglers Association, in the 70's, was the biggest in the world) to the tiny (4 of us once had the consent on a ½ acre farm pit…). Currently, I'm involved in one small, local club, and I'm really enjoying it.

I like being in a club. I like the fact I can really get to know a venue; not just depths and stuff like that, but the wildlife and the surroundings too. When you're in a club, you can turn up when you like, and just be there; you don't even have to fish. I once spent a few hours one evening throwing bread at some Carp, and didn't even get the rod out of the car. You can't do that on a day ticket water, and I learnt more about the behaviour of a surface feeding Carp that evening than I would have had I actually fished.

I like the fact you get to know the characters amongst your fellow members, and the fact that a certain pool is a no-no on a Monday because that's when so and so always goes and he talks, loudly, at whoever is in earshot.

I like the fact you get to know that a venue is a bad idea when the wind is in a particular direction, or perhaps after heavy rain when the levels are up. It's good to have that knowledge, and that feeling of belonging.

I hadn't been in a club for a while, and had considered joining this one for weeks. I consulted Her Ladyship, who has considerable experience of the Equine equivalent - the Riding Club, or the local branch of the Pony Club. She advised caution. 'You'll fall out with people', she said. She's probably right. She usually is. I joined anyway. And so far, the only people I've met have been tremendous company.

It's been an interesting experience, because I'm not a 'social ' angler. I don't go fishing for a chat. But I don't mind a passing conversation, or the exchange of a tip or suggestion. It helps the learning process; stimulates thought, which is a good thing for me - I like to learn, to think, to try new ideas. What is interesting, though, is an observation I've made about the people that fish… they *talk* … to *anyone*…

As I said, I'm not particularly sociable. I'm not rude, or ignorant, it's just that I enjoy my own company and am quite happy on my own, fishing, pondering, thinking. Cogitating, I think it's called. Here in Staffordshire, we're a naturally polite people, where total strangers, passing in the street, will wish each other a 'good morning' as they walk by.(Or an 'Ow do' in the north of the county). Contrast that with my experience a few years ago in the Capital, when I stood outside Euston station, lost, bewildered, and ignored completely by the hordes that swept by me, totally oblivious to my existence. It was horrible. The world, I thought, is like that now, a place where social media is vitally important and people no longer communicate by talking, where people simply don't care and have no time for thinking, or contemplation.

Sounds awful, and it is… except on a river bank, or alongside a lake, pond, or pool. Here is a place where conversations occur, where total strangers, united by a common goal of trying to catch a fish, will strike up a conversation as if they'd known each other for years. I bet there isn't an angler living that won't respond to an enquiring 'any good?' from a complete stranger. I don't think there is another social situation, anywhere, where 2 people will embark on a conversation with no previous knowledge of each other, with no introduction beforehand.

We teach our children, quite rightly, not to talk to strangers. And yet the shyest, most nervous child fishing his local farm pool or canal will confidently ask the adult fishing along the bank 'what did you catch that on?' and will expect, and receive, an answer.

This is a social phenomenon, and I'm not qualified to explain it. People from all walks of life will happily engage in conversation, and not give it a moments thought. It's a global phenomenon, too. On holiday in the Gambia many years ago, I borrowed a rod from a local and spent an evening sat on the beach, optimistically cranking in a big Rapala plug. After an hour I'd attracted a bit of an audience and Her Ladyship found me, later on, chatting happily to everyone, beer in one hand, rod in the other, and with a few small Butterfish on the sand to take back to the hotel. She was, to say the least, unimpressed. 'How come', she asked ' at dinner last night you spoke to no-one except me and the waitress. And yet, out here, with complete strangers, some of whom don't even speak English, you're the life and soul of the party...?' A good question!

You don't actually have to be fishing, by the way. We visited the Caribbean last year and I was approached at Grantley Adams airport by a gentleman who asked if I'd caught much lately. He'd spotted the logo of a well known tackle manufacturer on my shirt. Her Ladyship was not amused. 'Displeased' I think is the word. We were in 'Arrivals' and hadn't even started our holiday.

Izaak Walton had it right. In 1653, he wrote that we were all, irrespective of background or social standing, 'brothers of the angle'. That's it exactly. Spot on, Izaak, 350 years ago.

A Bit of Cane and a Bent Pin - a saga

Some years ago I wrote a piece for a website promoting fly fishing. I argued, (I hoped successfully), that it was cheaper than you thought, and that with no bait to buy, and only minimal tackle required, fly fishing for trout was cheaper than coarse fishing.

In the article I pointed out that a sense of proportion was required; obviously, I said, you could catch a Perch from your local canal with a garden cane and a worm dug from your garden. Not the cliched 'bent pin', but nearly so. I often reread stuff I wrote years ago. So I started to think - can you really catch Perch with a cane and a worm? Can you actually fish with real back to basics, hunter gatherer type stuff?

I've read lots of tales of anglers after the war using old tank aerials as poles. The 'roach pole' existed hundreds of years before reels and rods with rings on were thought of. So the idea of fishing with a cane and a fixed length of line wasn't 'going back to basics' at all, it was going back to the beginning. Thousands of years ago, in fact.

So I set myself a bit of a challenge. Go fishing, catch a fish, and use fundamental, basic kit, *without spending any money...*

I rummaged around behind the shed and found some old canes, originally intended for supporting beans, peas and suchlike. They were really quite stiff, and despite a natural taper, not flexible enough. If my Perch was anything more than a few ounces, I'd need some sort of shock absorbency. Perch jerk about a lot, thrashing around when they're hooked. Even a small one can put a bend in a rod. An unforgiving length of cane wasn't going to help.

Remember I'm trying to do this without spending anything. Of course modern pole elastic would work, tensioned correctly. But I also wanted something old fashioned, as well as free. Elastic bands looked promising for a while, and then deep thought (proper 'Thinking Fishing'!) produced a flash of inspiration. I cut a length off a willow branch, and spliced it into the end of the cane, creating what a pole fisherman would call a 'flick tip'.

(Technical Bit : the issue with poles and elastics, (especially in the early 80's when we were all learning and modern pole fishing was new) was that fish would be 'bumped off' on the strike. You'd respond to the float sinking, lift the pole, feel the fish… but the hook wouldn't 'set' and the fish would escape. The problem lay with the tip of the pole; it was stiff and unforgiving. The flick tip was the answer… a flexible length of tapered, hollow fibre glass or carbon, inserted into the end of the pole, and with the elastic running through it. The trick then, as it is now, was to get the tip to bend into the fish, pulling the hook home ('setting' the hook), before the elastic stretched out and did its stuff).

My willow flick tip should provide the necessary shock absorbency. I tied about 8 feet of 4lb nylon directly to the tip, and a size 16 eyed, barbless hook directly to that. Then I made a brew and sat back to think.

So far, so good. The nylon wasn't free as such, I nicked it from the reel I use for stick float fishing the rivers. The eyed hook was ancient 'old stock' I'd had for years. (Normally for a size 16 I'd always use a spade end hook whipped to a lighter length of fluorocarbon). So I'm still on zero expenditure and still on target!

More thought. Obviously I could now 'freeline' a bait, and the classic approach would be a small bit of floating bread crust. But that would probably attract a Carp, and anything bigger than a few ounces would smash my cane and willow outfit to bits. I had to fish at depth - so I'd need a float, and possibly some sort of weight.

Getting a float to 'cock' and sit upright in the traditional manner would require a properly made float (from a porcupine quill, or a goose or swan feather quill), and lead shot on the line to provide the weight to cock the float. Split lead shot would have to be bought, or borrowed, and Porcupines aren't exactly common in the Staffordshire countryside. Swans and Geese don't take kindly to being approached by anglers brandishing scissors, either.

I remembered reading a book when I was a teenager by the match angler Dickie Carr. One of the techniques he described was speed fishing for Bleak, on the Thames, using a short pole called a Whip. He used no shot or weight of any kind - Bleak feed on or near the surface, like Rudd - but to provide bite indication he used a matchstick, attached to the line a few feet above the hook. Would this work, I wondered, on a pond or canal, for Perch or Gudgeon?

Back to my Cane and Willow experiment... I tied a simple slip knot about 2 feet above the hook, inserted a match, and pulled it tight. Next step - bait. Specifically, worms.

An old trick for those of you that don't have the luxury of a farm muck heap to dig worms from, is to collect them from a lawn. If you don't have one of those to hand, a grass verge would do although passing motorists may wonder what you're up to, and question your sanity as they drive by. What you do is this - fill a bucket with cold water, and add a good slug of washing up liquid. Stir it gently to mix, you want a solution of washing up liquid, not bubbles or foam. Pour over your lawn, covering an area about 3 feet square. (That's a square metre if you're of a European disposition). Sit back and await developments – it's like magic. As the liquid soaks into the soil, worms, irritated by the chemicals in the washing up liquid, make their way to the surface to escape, where you simply pick them up, and put them in a bait box with some moss or grass cuttings. It's possible, especially after heavy rain on a waterlogged lawn, to collect dozens in a few minutes, including some fat, juicy lobworms ideal for big Perch or Chub.

So, now I had a makeshift cane/willow/matchstick outfit, and some free bait. Now I needed to try and catch something. A stretch of canal would be ideal but I realised my current club memberships didn't cover any of the local canals. Staffordshire is home to miles of towpath - the Birmingham/Fazeley, the Coventry, the Trent and Mersey, the Staffs and Worcester and the Cauldon canals spring to mind, plus all of the miles of the Potteries canal network. In fact, there are more miles of canal in Staffordshire than any other county - it was an ideal mode of transport for moving china clay into the Potteries and then the delicate bone china out again. I suppose I could have secured permission from somewhere, but being impatient I decided to try an old marl pit that I knew was full of small Perch and Roach. It also had the added advantage of being fairly deep close in - so I could fish under the rod tip - or rather, under the cane and willow tip…

I pulled a small redworm into pieces, slipped the hook into the smallest bit, and dropped it neatly into the edge, alongside some reeds. I'm not exaggerating when I say that only seconds had elapsed before the matchstick 'float' moved across the surface, sank, and the line tightened, pulling the willow flick tip around as the fish hooked itself. I lifted, the fish splashed across the surface and I swung in, not a Perch, but a small, perfectly formed, cheerful looking Crucian Carp. I was, I have to say, chuffed. A Perch would have been welcome, and rounded this article off nicely, but a Crucian? Well, Crucians are always special, and this one, caught on homemade tackle costing nothing, was even more so. I took a picture, slid it back, and went home smiling. Possibly the shortest fishing trip ever, and certainly one of the most memorable.

Cooking Fish

I am not a chef. At best, I cook. The basics I learnt from my mother, who was determined that her two sons should grow up being able to produce a hot meal for themselves. She still produces wonderful meals, and her chocolate cake is legendary.(I used to have a slice every day in my school lunchbox, which I would auction to the highest bidder. Over my 7 year secondary school career I made a fortune. Which I spent on bait and tackle!).

I thought it was appropriate to include some recipes in this book. There are a few fish based dishes I produce regularly; and believe me, if I can cook them, anyone can.

Grilled Lemon Sole (or Dover Sole)

My local supermarket often has these, and they are worth seeking out. Works with Plaice as well. Recently, the sea bass has become fashionable and is indeed delicious, but for me, the Sole is the tastiest of them all. Messing about with fancy sauces and accompaniments is just not necessary, in fact, I think it spoils things. This is how I do it…

Pat the fish dry with kitchen paper. Season with salt and pepper. Place the fish, dark skin side down, on a pyrex plate or similar, or in a frying pan that you can put under the grill. Dot the fish with some butter, and place under a hot grill. After a few minutes the flesh will start to brown and the edges crisp up. Turn the grill off, and as it cools, baste the fish with the melted butter. The thickest part of the fish should be just cooked through. Serve with a squeeze of lemon, the butter poured over the top, some bread to mop up the juices, and a glass or two of the driest, coldest white wine you can find. Chablis, if you can afford it. That's it - and it's perfect.

Asian Fish Parcels

I created this, in a panic, one evening when Her Ladyship reminded me we were going to some friends for dinner and I'd promised to provide the starter. It was a success and I've been cooking it ever since, mainly because the ingredients are stock things we always have in the fridge. You need a bag of frozen white fish fillets from the supermarket - Basa is OK, Cod is better, Sea bass would be good too.

Basically, you're creating a tin foil parcel per person. Place a fillet on an A4 sized piece of foil, (I do these on the worktop 4 at a time, it's easier), then add a knob of butter, salt and pepper, a squeeze of lime juice, some chopped chilli, ginger and garlic, and some chopped coriander. Add the squeezed out lime wedge to the fillet. Wrap up each parcel so that none of the liquid escapes. 15 minutes in the oven, or even on a Barbeque buried in the coals, and they're done. Each person gets a parcel, and there's no washing up. New Zealand Sauvignon Blanc with this one - although a cold beer works as well!

Poached smoked haddock

Not that horrible dyed yellow sort - just plain, good quality smoked haddock from a fishmonger or supermarket. Even frozen is OK if you can find it. You need a deep saute pan or a wok, filled with about an inch depth of milk. (25mm if you're metric). Add a few peppercorns, and a few bay leaves, and the fish. Set the pan on to a low heat.

Meanwhile, put some spinach, or chard, or pak choi, or a mixture of all three, into a pan on a medium heat, add some boiling water from a kettle, put the lid on, and leave it to steam and wilt; it'll take a few minutes. Remove the spinach to a colander, put the pan back on the heat with some fresh boiling water for the eggs. The fish should be almost cooked by now, poached in the hot milk; it should be just about to fall apart. Poach 1 egg per person (Duck eggs best, Hen eggs will do!), and while that's cooking squeeze the surplus water from the spinach, and season with salt, pepper and some butter. Put a handful of spinach on a plate, put the fish on top, and the poached egg on top of that. If you're feeling 'cheffy' you could add some sauce of some sort, maybe using some of the milk; I never bother. Chardonnay with this, I think!

Tiger Prawns with garlic, chilli and lemon

You know when you're walking along the harbour at sunset on holiday somewhere like the Canaries (Playa Blanca on Lanzarote springs to mind), and the air is filled with that smell of hot, garlicky seafood? This is how you get your kitchen to smell the same…

You need big, whole, uncooked Tiger or King Prawns, or 'crevettes'; 4 each for a starter, as many as you can afford for a main course… incidentally, this works with Squid as well, or a meaty fish like Monkfish.

Get a wok properly hot, on a hob or a BBQ. While it's heating up, rinse the prawns under the cold tap, and assemble some butter, vegetable oil, chopped garlic, chopped ginger, chopped parsley, a chopped chilli (or two!), lemon wedges, sea salt and pepper.

Add a splash of oil, and a big knob of butter, then the garlic, ginger and chilli. The smell will be amazing. Chuck the prawns in. Keep them moving, they'll take about 2 minutes to turn properly pink and cook through. Squeeze over the lemon, add parsley, salt and pepper, and eat while they're almost too hot to pick up. Nothing but a cold beer will do. The Asian ones are good - Tiger or Cobra.

Trout with Cinzano

This one takes a bit of doing, but it's worth it. You need a whole trout per two people, gutted and cleaned, ideally with the head still on but you can remove it if you have squeamish dining companions. The cavity needs seasoning with salt - lots of it. Stuff the fish with butter, lemon, and whatever green herbs you have to hand. Obviously tarragon is good, so is parsley, thyme, especially lemon thyme. Lay the fish on an enormous sheet of foil. Fold, and seal, the foil into a sort of rugby ball shape; you want lots of space inside. Before you seal up the last edge, add a glass of Cinzano, or dry Martini, or plain white wine. The idea is that the liquid evaporates and surrounds the fish, steaming it. About 20 minutes in a hot oven will be about right.

To serve this one, you need a sauce. Trout can be very dry, they need some help from a sauce or at least, some butter or lemon juice. What I do is pour the liquid from the foil bag into a saucepan, and boil it up so it reduces. I add some chopped parsley, and some creme fraiche, some pepper, warm it through, and then pour it over the fish.

Best wine? Not sure! Something Italian and white, Frascati maybe.

(Note : some rainbow trout can taste a bit earthy, or 'muddy'. Salt the fish, and soak overnight in salt water.

Rinse it under the tap before you prepare it. The earthiness magically disappears!)

Mum's Fish Pie

Every time I tried to cook this it was a disaster. The potato always dissolved into the sauce. I gave up trying, and asked Mum for advice. The sauce, and the potato have to be *cold,* otherwise it doesn't work.

Make mashed potato in the usual way, with lots of butter and salt added. Let it cool - better still, chill it in the fridge. I use about 4 big potatoes; nothing worse than not quite having enough to cover the fish. Make a basic parsley sauce (I use a packet one!) and pour it into a suitable ovenproof dish. ¾ pint of sauce should come about ⅓ of the way up the sides of the dish. Add the fish to the sauce (don't worry about it being uncooked – it's going into the oven!). You need a good mixture of fish, and some supermarkets do 'fish pie mix', which is OK, but I try to use some salmon or trout, some white fish like cod, some prawns or mussels, and some smoked haddock. Squid is good as well. Also worth adding is a handful of frozen peas.

Add the cold mash on top a spoonful at a time, until you've covered it. Then into a hot oven until the potato is browning and the sauce bubbling away underneath.

Pinot Grigio please!

Like I said, I'm not a chef - but the recipes are simple enough, and they're tasty, and worth doing.

Some Quotations

It isn't just me that thinks about his (or her) fishing. Described by Izaak Walton as 'the contemplative man's recreation', no other sport lends itself so well to accompanied, almost idle cogitation.

Some of the following quotes are reproduced mainly because they made me smile, and some because as you'd expect, they made me think; also because every angler, without exception, would agree with every word…

Fishing is only an addiction if you're trying to give it up…

A bad day's fishing is better than a good day's work.

Everyone should believe in something. I believe I'll go fishing…

My biggest fear is that when I die, my wife will sell my fishing tackle for what I told her I paid for it…

Fishing is much more than fish. It is the great occasion when we may return to the fine simplicity of our forefathers. (H.Hoover)

I have fished through fishless days that I remember happily, without regret.

Fly Fishing for Trout is like raising children. You never know what's coming next.

I go fishing... not to lose myself, but to find myself...

The solution to any problem, work, love, money,, whatever... is to go fishing. The bigger the problem, the longer the trip should be.

There is a certain something in angling, that produces a serenity of mind...

Many go fishing all their lives without ever knowing that it is not just the fish they are after...

Rivers and the inhabitants of the watery elements are made for wise men to contemplate and for fools to pass by without consideration... (Izaak Walton)

The true fisherman approaches the first day of the fishing season with the sense of awe and wonder of a child approaching Christmas.

I am not against Golf. I suspect it keeps armies of the unworthy from discovering Trout...

36867076R00101

Printed in Poland
by Amazon Fulfillment
Poland Sp. z o.o., Wrocław